BECOMING AN OVERCOMER BY DEFEATING YOUR ENEMIES!

DON DAY

ISBN: 978-1-66640-622-1

CONTENTS

FOREWORD

Proverbs 21:31 (NIV)

The horse is made ready for the day of battle, but victory rests with the Lord.

The battles of life are a certainty, victory is optional. In *Becoming an Overcomer by Defeating Your Enemies* the reader is given an opportunity to plot a course for victory. Life is more difficult than I would prefer. Each life stage is filled with challenge and opportunity.

I have known Don Day for more than two decades. We have walked together through a variety of challenges and miracles. I have watched Don negotiate the collapse of financial markets and celebrate the arrival of grandchildren. He has faced disaster and blessing with equal dignity. However, a direct assault on his physical health presented a new kind of adversary. I am not surprised that Don has responded with an assertive faith.

Anyone who is walking through a shadowed valley can find a response point in this book. It affords each of us the opportunity to imagine an outcome that enriches our lives and helps deliver us from victim status. The book of Revelation is often considered the most intimidating of all the books in Scripture. It describes the closing scenes of this age, the arrival of the King and God's Judgment of this present world order. All of the promises in the book of Revelation are presented to the "one who overcomes." Overcoming is not an optional response to life. It is required if we are to experience God's best. Do not allow the challenges of life to rob you of your destiny, accept the assignment to grow and know that victory rests with the Lord as we learn to live our faith each day. Our God is faithful!

Pastor Allen Jackson

CHAPTER 1

THE ONLY EASY DAY WAS YESTERDAY

"You haven't had a stroke; you're in the beginning stages of Parkinson's disease."

Parkinson's disease! How can that be possible? I was the only fifty-something on the court playing against twenty-and-thirty-somethings. When a young guard dribbled by me, I'd go for the steal and get it! That is, until I got a partial tear of my Achilles tendon. After five months of wearing a cast, being in a walking boot, and doing physical therapy, I was finally released for normal activities.

Two weeks later I was in Scottsdale, Arizona on a twelve-day trip when, on day two, I was walking up the stairs and heard a loud pop and felt like I'd been shot in the bottom of my leg. Results: Full tear of the Achilles tendon. I asked my wife, Shelly, to go and purchase every roll of KT Athletic tape she could find in Scottsdale. She found thirty-eight rolls, which I used to make a temporary cast. While my foot felt disconnected from my leg, the tape cast made life a little more bearable.

One day a client sent me a video from one of my speaking events, a year after I had fully recovered following Achilles surgery and physical therapy. As I watched the video, I noticed I never moved my right hand. It appeared as though my right wrist had been glued to my belt. I also noticed how diminished my right side was. My arm didn't swing when I walked, nor did I gesture with it during the entire speaking event. My first thought was that I must have had a stroke.

Two weeks later I was at my annual physical and told my primary care physician about the video and my thoughts about having a stroke. My doctor asked me a few questions and ran me through a few tests and told me something that rocked my world: "You haven't had a stroke; you're in the beginning stages of Parkinson's disease."

I was in shock. How could this be?

That's when the enemy attacked. Meanwhile, my doctor said, "Parkinson's won't kill you, but you will die with it. It's a cruel disease and we don't have a cure."

This only triggered more inward attacks from the enemy, anger, and thoughts of *Why me? What have I done to deserve this? I work out regularly and I'm an avid runner and I stay in shape. My physical results are always fantastic; why me?*

Yet more attacks with anxiety, indecision, more fear, and self-sabotage. Telling my family was difficult to say the least. They had concerns and more questions than I had answers. I think in many ways illness is harder on the family than the patient. I wanted to be strong in front of them, but I was sinking in the quicksand of unbelief and fear. We all needed answers.

I made an appointment with a neurologist who was local to me. He ordered magnetic resonance imaging (MRI) of my brain, and while there was evidence that I did indeed have a brain—which had been questioned by some in my life—there was no evidence that I had suffered a stroke. After more tests and evaluation came the verdict: Without a doubt I had Parkinson's disease. My mind couldn't accept this medical diagnosis. It still didn't make sense. They had to be wrong. There must be some mistake. This was not possible.

So, I made an appointment with Vanderbilt Health Parkinson's Center in Nashville, Tennessee. Again, after several tests and physical evaluation, the team announced that I had Parkinson's disease.

The enemy then presented the "fight or flight" option to me. First, I just wanted to run away and think. By then, I was certain of my diagnosis, but under that mental and spiritual attack I couldn't think straight. My mind raced. I entered the land of "what-ifs."

My experience grappling with the enemy that day reminded me of what I knew about him: I have learned that when you receive a bad diagnosis or tragic news, he will use these as weapons to knock you off your path. Why does he use them? Because they work on us, and he knows just where to find us.

As a believer and follower of Jesus, I believe we live in two spiritual time zones: Time and Eternity. I refer to *Time* as our life "under the sun" and *Eternity* as life "under the Son." In our Time, we are on the path to Eternity while we fulfill God's plan and purposes. But I encourage you to be aware that the enemy always wants to knock us off the path to Eternity.

That day, as I sat in my car replaying the confirming news of the diagnosis in my mind, I tried to make sense of it all, but again my mind raced from one thought to another. I was stuck in the middle of a fight for my life, but one thing became very clear to me when I heard a voice say: "With men this is impossible, but with God all things are possible." Matthew 19:26 (NKJV) Immediately, Philippians 4:13 came to my mind, "I can do all things through Him who strengthens me." (ESV)

He said I can do *all* things—not a few things, not most things, but *all* things.

Let the fight begin, I thought, *I'm all in!*

Point of Attack (POA)

It is my hope that this book will teach you how to outwit and defeat your enemies. These pages are not filled with academic theory, but with real-life experience from a battle I fight every day, one day at a time. Stick with me through this journey and you, too, will have the formula to change your future life conditions and defeat every enemy that comes against you. You can, you will, and you must become an overcomer. You can do all things!

One way to overcome an enemy attack, whether personal, spiritual, or professional, is to know how to get off the target. In the military, we prepare for what to do if we are ever caught in an ambush, and that is to find the Point of Attack (POA), which is also called "X." The POA, or X, is where the enemy has the best vantage point and the best ability to inflict a massive assault to completely destroy you. The first thing you must do when caught in an ambush is to get off of X, the Point of Attack, if you want to survive.

In life, the enemy—Satan—comes to steal, kill, and destroy you, so he prowls around looking for the best place to attack you—his POA. I have found that his favorite places to assault are in health, family, and finances. He knows where you are most vulnerable. He attacks you there.

It's hard to think rationally when you are under attack. It's hard to process information and make decisions when you are attacked, in shock, disoriented, and in pain. You must calm and control your mind and get off the POA, or X, as quickly as possible.

To get off the POA you have to make decisions, move, or take action. One of those decisions is whether you are going to be overcome or to be an overcomer.

The choices and decisions we make will affect us far more than any circumstances that may befall us. Never allow anyone to look down on you or pity you or feel sorry for you and your circumstances. You aren't stuck under circumstances, you are an overcomer! You are still among the living; you are still standing, and you are in control of how you respond to what happens to you.

The enemy wants to devastate you, to overwhelm you, to destroy your will and your mind, and to make it impossible for you to escape. As Jesus said in John 16:33, "In this world you will have trouble … be of good cheer I have overcome the world." With men things seem impossible, but with God *all* things are possible.

Becoming an Overcomer Requires a No-Excuses Attitude and Never-Give-Up Mentality

Let's begin with the number one enemy of the people: fear! Fear can be brutal. You see, fear grows and gains momentum and power with the passing of time. Face fear early and often while it's small or new.

Unmanaged fear can cause you to make poor decisions, or worse yet, it can paralyze you so that you make no decision at all. Fear will make you feel stuck, hopeless, and helpless. Some begin to blame others for their circumstance while others get angry and curse God and anyone else in the line of fire.

As you face challenges and succumb to fear, you may find yourself asking, "Why me?" But beware of the blame game. It only drags you down, exhausts you emotionally, and eats up time, which grows the fear. The blame game or victim mentality is a tactic from the enemy to knock you off the path to

Eternity. Don't fall for it. He wants you to cast blame, to feel weak and small. But the Bible says, "For God has not given us a spirit of fear and timidity, but of power, love, and self-discipline." 2 Timothy 1:7 (NLT) Remember that you have the power of God's strength to help you overcome fear. He equips us to fight giants through two promises for us: First, He will always be with us; secondly, He will empower us to defeat the enemy.

In the midst of a fear storm, our emotions can threaten to unseat these promises in our hearts and minds. Some people compare these feelings to waves at the beach. The first waves may knock you off your feet, then your footing becomes a little stronger. But at any time a large wave can suddenly come back and knock you off your feet again. The waves of emotions may not hit in any particular order, but they will surely return to attack you again and again. Crucially, you must get off the POA—get off of the X. Even as we waver, God's promises remain.

Take Action

Inaction breeds doubt and fear. Action breeds confidence and courage. In this book you will learn to employ strategies to defeat the tactics from the enemy, including his propensity to play upon your fear. I encourage you to keep trying. You must keep chasing the dream or you may never find it. This is where your faith will kick in if you don't lose it—in a moment when you, like me, will vow to yourself, *Let the fight begin… I'm all in!*

Here are some concrete actions that may help you regain your sense of power when you feel the enemy attack through fear:

- Identify what fear is. Fear, and nothing more.

- Take some time to calm down. It's impossible to think clearly when you're flooded with fear, anxiety, or what-ifs. The first thing to do is take a quick time-out so you can physically calm down.
- Think. Fear means we are losing or have already lost our ability to think. Take time to think about why you are afraid and how you will overcome the feeling. Being overcome is not an option. You must go on the attack and must not hunker down in fear. Remind yourself of your power through God. 2 Timothy 1:7
- Face the fear. Know that you need to attack fear now while it's small. Avoiding fear only makes it scarier. Regardless of your fear, if you face it, it will start to diminish.
- Know that fear may wax and wane. You might feel strong today and scared tomorrow. This is normal. Continue to fight your fear. The fear will fade.

What fear does when it builds its power over us is to lock up our hands and feet to keep us from doing the simplest things of life—working, playing, dressing, spending time with our families, and serving God. Never give in to the bondage and chains of fear. Instead, take action toward building a mindset that overcomes fear.

Parkinson's Disease Is the Gift That Keeps On Taking!

- It steals your mobility. You move slower and your gait changes. You lose your balance and that makes you slow down even more. It robs you of your good posture. You begin to lean over and shuffle as you walk and battle to find your new center of gravity. Everything slows down. Your depth perception diminishes.

- Tremors and spasms begin and get worse. Your dexterity diminishes. Difficulty doing simple tasks like tying shoes or buttoning shirts becomes frustrating and embarrassing to the patient. I experience this from time to time and when I do I find myself responding in the same way. I will button and unbutton my clothes ten times just to prove *I can. I will. I must. I will not quit.*
- It attacks your voice, which becomes weak and different. On occasion you may slur the words you speak, making it more difficult for others to understand or hear you. If this happens just do the following: Slow down, think before you speak, swallow, and then use the right amount of force to say what you want. Parkinson's will continue to attack, we just need to fight back. We must be intentional. Never give up. So many are depending on you.
- Swallowing becomes more difficult. You must slow down when you are eating and watch what you eat to keep from choking. Your family and friends should learn cardiopulmonary resuscitation (CPR) and how to perform the Heimlich maneuver in case you need it.
- It can change your personality. You become quieter and more removed. Your facial expressions fade and are replaced with a blank stare. Therefore, we must be intentional now with our responses and expressions.
- You become more rigid and stiff. This causes you to sit more and you eventually atrophy in your legs, which makes you less mobile. This is a death trap. Keep moving.

Fight or Flight

So, I choose to fight.

- I work out every day.
- I ride my Peloton three or four days per week.
- I work with a trainer three times a week on balance and mobility and stretching for flexibility.
- I have resumed running three to five miles several days a week and am walking the same.
- I do intravenous (IV) therapy to improve my hydration.

Remember *who* you are and *whose* you are.

Ask the Holy Spirit to help you.

Encourage yourself.

Refuse to speak curses over your life. Stop saying "I can't" or "I will never" and any other quitter slang you might come up with. Don't let others speak negativity into your life. Don't listen to the discouraging words about someone's uncle, sister, or friend who has Parkinson's and who is now unable to care for themselves. Never let anyone pity or feel sorry for you. You are an overcomer. You are winning the battle. You are to be admired.

CHAPTER 2

WE SUFFER MORE IN WORRY THAN IN REALITY!

"Do not be anxious about anything, but in every situation, by prayer and petition, with thanksgiving, present your requests to God. And the peace of God, which transcends all understanding, will guard your hearts and your minds in Christ Jesus." Philippians 4:6-7 (NIV)

Depending on who you believe, it has now been defined that the average lifespan for an average person is seventy-eight years. On average, twenty-eight of those years will be spent sleeping, and as many as seven of those sleeping years are spent lying awake at night with worry.

The older I get and the more I reflect on my life, I wish I'd worried less. I've come to recognize that worry isn't worth the cost of stress, lost sleep, fatigue, problems, loss of energy, and feelings of helplessness.

There is much to worry about. We worry about our family, career, money, retirement, crime, politics, health, friends, relationships, the unknown, and about a million other things.

When my daughter first started driving, like many new drivers, she had a few minor accidents. One evening she went out with a few friends and she was the driver. Sometime later my wife woke me up saying, "Something is wrong!" Our daughter hadn't answered her cell phone and hadn't responded to text messages.

"She may have had an accident!" my wife said.

I'm not much of a worrier so I assured her our daughter was fine—she was probably having fun and not checking her phone. "You worry too much," I said, and I tried to go back to sleep. But as I lay there my mind started thinking, *She has had a few accidents; she is with her friends and they may be talking, laughing, and listening to music and not paying attention while driving.* I said, "Don't just sit there, start calling the hospitals and her friends—she could be lying in a ditch!" Minutes later our daughter checked in and all was fine. Most of what we worry about never happens!

Ways to Deal with Worry, Anxiety, and Fear

- Fear God and nothing else. If you have a healthy fear of God, you need fear nothing else.
- Know your value to God.
- Trust the Holy Spirit.
- Don't hold a pity party. Don't send or accept invitations to a pity party.
- Don't miss the purpose of life.

We can only have one thought at a time. Can you train yourself to worry less? Below you'll find two of my favorite tips for worrying less.

- Wait to worry. Procrastinate. Put worrying off till tomorrow or next week. Decide you will wait to worry.

It's been defined that 90 percent of what we worry about never ever happens. So, wait it out.

- Interrupt the worry pattern. Keep busy. If you worry excessively, find activities that can easily distract your thought process. One way is to get up and get moving—exercise is a natural way to break the worry cycle because it releases endorphins, which relieve tension and stress, boost energy, and enhance your sense of well-being.

DOUBT

"I've learned nothing external has any power over me."

James 1:6, describes the man who doubts as "a wave of the sea that is driven and tossed by the wind." (NIV) When you are about to attempt something new and you hesitate, doubt arrives on your doorstep. Don't answer the door.

- Doubt destroys your motivation and momentum. When your motivation is destroyed, you will never get out of the boat to walk on the water or take risks. The attacks against you will rage on with no retaliation from you because you allow doubt to stop you and knock you off the path. Doubt will destroy your momentum and your confidence.
- Seeds of doubt are planted in your mind, which will spread to every area of your faith. Doubt is extremely contagious and dangerous. Dispose of doubtful thoughts immediately before they grow and spread.
- The enemy wants to silence you and knock you off your path. His weapon in this case is doubt.

Anger

When I was diagnosed with Parkinson's I wondered, *Why did this happen to me? I'm a good person, I am a believer and follower of Jesus Christ as Lord. I'm generous, compassionate, kind, handsome, oh yeah … and humble! Why has God allowed this to happen to me?*

I found myself getting angry at myself, my family, the team at work—I was pretty much mad and angry, period. This is not my personality. I'm usually upbeat, positive, and looking at the stuff going right, not the stuff going wrong.

Our enemy, Satan, tells us that our problems are our fault and that they exist because of all the bad things we've done. We deserve the bad diagnosis or tragic news. There is no way out—wrong! We serve a healing God.

I learned we can blame God, ask God hard questions, critique his job performance, or be angry with God, but we must always *believe* in God.

He is in charge of everything. He allowed this disease to come to me. Now is the time to seek Him and invest my time working for His plan and purposes and not waste time seeking my relief. I know God knows what is best for me and His plan—I have to trust Him and overcome so that others can witness His power and persevere.

When I entered the Air Force, I wondered how I could succeed in the training for a school where 60 percent fail. The answer was easy and has served me well these last forty-six years: Don't Quit! Never give up. Don't stop. Never ring the bell.

Fight Against Fear, Worry, and Doubt with the Powerful Truth from God's Word

All of us will experience worry, doubt, fear, and anxiety during our life under the sun. I think we should be grateful that **God planned ahead for when we would struggle with trouble** and challenges during our life in Time. His Word is jam-packed with scriptures that combat and neutralize worry, doubt, fear, and anxiety.

I've learned that, at all times in this life, we will either be in a challenge, coming out of a challenge, or getting ready for the next challenge. This is normal. Expect the unexpected.

During the most challenging times we must speak and pray scripture to the challenge and to our Lord. We should claim God's Word and promises. Just as Isaiah 55:11 says, "So is my word that goes out from my mouth: It will not return to me empty but will accomplish what I desire and achieve the purpose for which I sent it." (NIV)

Below are my favorite scriptures to use against fear, worry, and doubt. Memorize them so you are loaded and ready when the enemy attacks. When you claim and use these scriptures, the enemy must flee.

"A life well-lived after a bad diagnosis or tragic news."

- **Philippians 4:6-7:** "Don't worry about anything; instead, pray about everything. Tell God what you need, and thank Him for all He has done. Then you will experience God's peace, which exceeds anything we can understand. His peace will guard your hearts and minds as you live in Christ Jesus" (NLT).
- **Matthew 6:34:** "Therefore do not worry about tomorrow, for tomorrow will worry about itself. Each day has enough trouble of its own." (NIV)

- **Deuteronomy 31:6:** "Be strong and courageous. Do not fear or be in dread of them, for it is the Lord your God who goes with you. He will not leave you or forsake you." (ESV)
- **John 14:1:** "Let not your hearts be troubled. Believe in God; believe also in me." (ESV)
- **John 14:27**: "I am leaving you with a gift–peace of mind and heart. And the peace I give is a gift the world cannot give. So don't be troubled or afraid." (NLT)
- **Psalm 34:4:** "I sought the Lord, and he answered me; he delivered me from all my fears." (NIV)
- **Joshua 1:9:** "Have I not commanded you? Be strong and courageous. Do not be frightened, and do not be dismayed, for the Lord your God is with you wherever you go." (ESV)
- **Psalm 27:1:** "The Lord is my light and my salvation; whom shall I fear? The Lord is the stronghold of my life; of whom shall I be afraid?" (ESV)
- **1 Peter 5:6-9:** "So humble yourselves under the mighty power of God, and at the right time He will lift you up in honor. Give all your worries and cares to God, for He cares about you. Stay alert! Watch out for your great enemy, the devil. He prowls around like a roaring lion, looking for someone to devour. Stand firm against him, and be strong in your faith. Remember that your Christian brothers and sisters all over the world are going through the same kind of suffering you are." (NLT)
- **Psalm 23:4:** "Even when I walk through the darkest valley, I will not be afraid, for you are close beside me. Your rod and your staff protect and comfort me." (NLT)

CHAPTER 3

WE ARE OUR OWN WORST ENEMY

Self-sabotage is when people do (or don't do) things that block their success or prevent them from reaching and exceeding their goals. It can happen consciously or unconsciously. These self-sabotaging behaviors can affect our personal and professional success, as well as our mental health.

Self-sabotaging behavior often comes as the result of low self-esteem, negative self-talk, negative emotions, a bad diagnosis, and bad news.

Sometimes a bad diagnosis or bad news will spin us into a negative nosedive. This is self-sabotage. It can and often does leave us hopeless. This is another tool the enemy uses to knock you off the path.

People react differently to a terminal diagnosis or bad news. Some people go silent. They can't believe what they are hearing, and they don't know what to say or do. Others start to cry or lose control and feel as though they won't be able to survive. Some people become angry and scared. They blame God and others. Some people give up and are overcome and overwhelmed. Others seek more medical opinions and search all available information and ideas to combat the illness or bad news with.

We don't know why God allows these bad things to happen to good people. We know that the rain falls on the just and unjust, and we also know that He is creator and knows what's best. I trust Him. You can trust Him, too.

Turning away from God during big trouble is the last thing we should do, and having you do so is another way the enemy wants to knock you off the path. Don't do it. God is our only answer for big trouble. Draw closer to the Holy Spirit. He will comfort you and direct your steps. Invite the Holy Spirit into all of your decisions and plans.

I'm glad God gives second chances! I have made plenty of mistakes in my life. I'm certainly glad God didn't give up on me, but instead kept coming back until I surrendered and let Him have His way with my life. I daily give praise to God for His patience, mercy, and second chances.

God gave Jonah a second chance. Many times, like Jonah, we find ourselves in need of a second chance. You know the times I'm talking about. Times we rebel against God because we didn't get our way or we think life was unfair to us. *Why me?* The times we turned our backs on God in anger or selfish ambition. We build our plan and ask Him to bless it. We forget we serve at His pleasure and His plan not ours. Don't go into battle with the enemy without the power of God!

These are the times when we have made a total disaster of our lives and those times when, because we rebelled against God, He had to get our attention the hard way.

God used a storm and three days and nights in the belly of a whale to get Jonah's attention.

What is He using to get your attention? Has He gotten it yet? If He has, are you taking advantage of that second chance? How?

Are you awake and vigilant to help and encourage others? Are you responsible to God for another chance? How?

When We Are Spiritually Asleep...People Are in Danger.

"All the sailors were afraid and each cried out to his own God. And they threw the cargo into the sea to lighten the ship.

"But Jonah had gone below deck, where he lay down and fell into a deep sleep. The captain went to him and said, 'How can you sleep? Get up and call on your God! Maybe he will take notice of us so that we will not perish." Jonah 1:5-6 (NIV)

Running from God exhausted Jonah physically and emotionally, so, he slept during a storm. He was asleep both physically and spiritually. He was unaware and unconcerned.

We often joke about people falling asleep in church, but the real tragedy is when we are asleep spiritually. You can't defeat the enemy attacks when you are asleep and unaware.

The Bible also reminds us of this: "So then, let us not be like others, who are asleep, but let us be awake and sober. 1 Thessalonians 5:6 (NIV) Be vigilant and ready to defend these enemy attacks against you. You need God in the storms of life. Remember you are an overcomer. You will not stop. You can do it. Your family and others are counting on you to overcome!

Our Enemy Never Sleeps.

"But while everyone was sleeping, his enemy came and sowed weeds among the wheat, and went away." Matthew 13:25 (NIV)

"How long will you lie there, you sluggard? When will you get up from your sleep? A little sleep, a little slumber, a little folding of the hands to rest—and poverty will come on you like a thief and scarcity like an armed man." Proverbs 6:9-11 (NIV)

We endanger our life and other people's lives by our actions and inactions.

"The sea was getting rougher and rougher. So, they asked him, 'What should we do to you to make the sea calm down for us?'" Jonah 1:11 (NIV)

When we follow the downward spiral, we usually carry others with us.

"Now the Lord provided a huge fish to swallow Jonah, and Jonah was in the belly of the fish three days and three nights." (Jonah 1:17, NIV)

If we are acting like a spiritual infant, someone who may be weaker than us could be watching, and their lives might be changed forever for the worst. Be the example of an overcomer.

We are swallowed up by the whales of our own making. What you choose to believe makes all the difference. Your choices make a difference.

We get a second chance when we realize we have blown it and admit it.

'Pick me up and throw me into the sea,' he replied, 'and it will become calm. I know that it is my fault that this great storm has come upon you.' (Jonah 1:12, NIV)

WE PRAY AND REPENT

"From inside the fish Jonah prayed to the LORD his God. He said: 'In my distress I called to the LORD and he answered me. From deep in the realm of the dead I called for help and you listened to my cry.'" Jonah 2:1-2 (NIV)

TO REVIEW:

- We put ourselves in the place of getting a second chance when we pour out our heart to the God. Regardless of our current circumstance we must seek God. He is the only one who can help.
- He already knows all about us; He wants us to confess that we are sinners.
- Often times, it is the whales of our life that drive us back to God. Your whale might be a bad diagnosis or tragic news. Seek God.

Chapter 4

INDECISION AFTER THE ATTACK

"Every Good and Bad Thing That Has Happened in Your Life Is Because Something Changed."

The decisions and choices we make affect us far more than any circumstance or condition we may experience. Even this situation will come to pass, not stay.

Not every attack nor every bad thing is from the enemy, Satan. We are fully capable of disobedience, selfish ambition, lying, and practicing many types of sin, all on our own. Then we blame God and others.

The Armor of God (Spiritual Warfare)

"Finally, be strong in the Lord and in His mighty power. Put on the full armor of God, so that you can take your stand against the devil's schemes. For our struggle is not against flesh and blood, but against the rulers, against the authorities, against the powers of this dark world and against the spiritual forces of evil in the heavenly realms." Ephesians 6:10-12 (NIV)

> "I know your deeds, that you are neither cold nor hot. I wish you were either one or the other! So, because you are lukewarm—neither hot nor cold—I am about to spit you out of my mouth." Revelation 3:15-16 (NIV)

Indecision usually shows up with stress, anxiety, and depression and it can severely impact your ability to function in life. Because if you are indecisive, someone else—the enemy—will decide on your behalf. It's called bondage. Guard against it.

When you are knocked down with bad news or a bad diagnosis, you can become indecisive and get further bogged down in the bondage making it almost impossible to think your way out. This is where faith has to kick in, which requires the power of the Holy Spirit. You will need the power to overcome. You can't do it alone. Don't justify, quit, or deceive yourself. You can't outthink evil. Invite the power of the Holy Spirit often.

The Unmatched Power of the Holy Spirit

> "And you shall receive power when the Holy Spirit has come upon you; and you shall be my witnesses in Jerusalem and in all Judea and Samaria and to the end of the Earth." Acts 1:8

A child of God needs the enabling power of the Holy Spirit to live victoriously and defeat the enemy. The power of God is vital for the challenges that we will face. This power that Jesus speaks about is not a one-time event. In fact, the Bible talks about how the disciples repeatedly sought God for refreshing.

The Holy Spirit plays many roles. In John 14, for example, Jesus says the Holy Spirit will comfort us when we're hurting. "I will not leave you as orphans," Jesus says (14:18), promising that the Spirit will bring us peace (14:27).

Jesus also says the Spirit will help us recall the things we've learned about God (14:26)—which also means the Spirit will help us when we tell others about our faith.

In John 16, Jesus refers to the Spirit as a "Counselor" who will guide us in our everyday lives. One way he'll guide us is by convicting us of sin (16:8). God wants us to get rid of the things that displease him, and the only way to identify those things is to be convicted by the Spirit. The Spirit works to make us aware of sin in our lives so we can take action to repent.

Romans 8 tells us the Spirit will help us stop sinning and do the things that please God. The Spirit helps us pray (8:26). We've all gone to God and said, "Lord, I'm just not sure how to pray or what to say." The Holy Spirit helps us in those times and actually intercedes for us, saying the prayers *for* us directly to the Lord.

The Holy Spirit can't and won't do *all* the work for us. We're still responsible to do our part—especially to consistently read our Bibles and pray, asking the Spirit to show us the truth then act.

It's important to remember that the Spirit will not prompt us to do anything that goes against Scripture. We need to make sure we're listening to the voice of the Holy Spirit, not the voice of our own desires. And we know which is which by checking this voice against the truth of God's Word.

Acts 2:4 speaks of believers who were "filled with the Holy Spirit." And after receiving this power, they came back to God to be refreshed against the new threats that they were facing. Stay close to God and the Holy Spirit.

The apostle Paul wrote, "... the Spirit also helps our weakness; for we do not know what to pray as we should, but the Spirit Himself intercedes for us with groanings too deep for words; and He who searches the hearts knows what the mind of the Spirit is, because He intercedes for the saints according to the *will* of God." Romans 8:26-27 (NASB).

What is our weakness in prayer? At times we do not know how to fully express our desires, and perhaps at times we don't realize what we need. Sometimes we are so exhausted—in spirit, mind, and body—from the enemy attacks that we can hardly muster the energy to open our mouth. There are instances when discouragement and depression has taken such a strong hold of our heart that we cannot imagine a way out of our painful condition, and all we can ask is for the Father to help us. Through that help is how we become overcomers.

Now that you know you need the power of the Holy Spirit, here are five ways to receive it:

1. **Immerse yourself in the Word of God.** God equips you with His power to enable you to proclaim His Word successfully. It is important that we must immerse ourselves in His Word, which is life. In John 6:63 Jesus said, "It is the Spirit that gives life, the flesh is of no avail; the words that I have spoken to you are Spirit and life." (NIV)

   The Bible is the Word of God and when you read it, you are reading the life-giving power of the Spirit. By soaking in God's Word, we activate our faith that helps us walk in the power of the Holy Spirit in all circumstances.

   At every POA, we must take action. The Holy Spirit helps empower us to do just that. The only requirement is to believe and step out in faith. Many times, in the face of fear.
2. **Pursue God's face.** Daily we need to seek the face of God diligently and pursue His presence relentlessly. The more we wait on God, the more we renew power to walk this life in the Spirit. Acts 1:13 says, "All these with one accord were devoting themselves to prayer …" It was only when

the disciples devoted themselves to prayer in Jerusalem during the ten days of waiting in the upper room that the power of the Holy Spirit fell on them.

We must also take time every day to withdraw from the Weapons of Mass Distraction around us to seek His face. You must identify your Weapons of Mass Distraction. They can be social media, emails, shopping on Amazon or any number of other things. Get them under control. The Bible says Jesus came full of power after his forty days of fasting. Fasting and prayer with undivided attention is the key to receiving God's power.

3. **Believe and claim the promise in the Word of God.** "It is impossible to please God without faith." Hebrews 11:6 (NLT) We cannot walk in the power of the Holy Spirit if we do not walk by faith. We need to develop a child-like faith to walk in the power of God. This is the path to becoming an overcomer.

   In Luke 11:13, Jesus says to his disciples, "If you then, who are evil, know how to give good things to your children, how much more will the heavenly Father give the Holy Spirit to those who ask Him!" (ESV) Start by asking today! Ask God to increase your faith. The Lord desires to fill you with His power.
4. **Abide in him.** Here's an important phase that we tend to forget. It is not enough that you receive God's power once. We need to continue to dwell in Him. You need to take time to study the Word and abide in it. John 14 is a chapter that you should take extended time to meditate, pray and believe.
5. **Love one another.** Jesus gives the commandment in John 15:12 that we should love one another as he has loved us. Jesus came for the sick.

So, let us immerse ourselves in the Word and put to death every unbelief and commit ourselves to fast and pray for His power to manifest through our lives. Continue pursuing God every single day of our lives. Live to make His name lifted up in all the Earth!

When you are fighting your battle, it is normal that you will become exhausted and afraid. This is normal but Satan will try to explode your fear and exhaustion into you quitting and knock you off your path. Be careful to not be overcome.

Angels Go to Work when God's Servants Are Tired, Hungry, or Afraid

Look, God has allowed this "ambush attack" to happen to you. I don't know why, but I know He knows what's best. I trust Him and so can you. In the fight you will become exhausted, tired, afraid, and indecisive. God is able to rescue you—have faith and don't quit. You are an overcomer! Stay on the path.

"Elijah was afraid and ran for his life … 'I have had enough, Lord,' he said. 'Take my life; I am no better than my ancestors.' Then he lay down under the tree and fell asleep. All at once an angel touched him and said, 'Get up and eat.' He looked around, and there by his head was a cake of bread baked over hot coals, and a jar of water. He ate and drank and then lay down again. The angel of the Lord came back a second time and touched him and said, 'Get up and eat, for the journey is too much for you.'" 1 Kings 19:3, 5-7 (NIV)

"The angel of the Lord said to Elijah, 'Go down with him; do not be afraid of him.' So, Elijah got up and went down with him to the king." 2 Kings 1:15 (NIV)

Lesson learned from the ambush attack.

"The angel of the Lord encamps around those who fear him, and he delivers them." Psalm 34:7 (NIV)

Chapter 5

PERSEVERE, PERSIST, ENDURE WITHOUT EXCEPTION

Dora Tomchak's Story: Overcomer Diagnosed with Triple-Positive Breast Cancer 11/5/21

I'd describe myself as a fairly driven individual. Started off in the corporate world, then swapped over to non-profit in 2000 at age thirty-three to be an event planner for a large interdenominational church. I was married for twenty-six years and had two children and two grandchildren, then I divorced at age fifty. I've always seen myself as the strong one, the problem-solver. So, a cancer diagnosis I had no control over put me in a very unfamiliar position.

What was your immediate response to your health diagnosis or bad news?

Deep down, I knew something was not right. I began mammogram screenings several years prior, and it was never a simple "see you next year" process. I always got called back for additional testing, resulting in weeks of stress each year. I dreaded the initial screening, then knowing it would be followed by more tests. This time seemed different—I kept delaying the appointment, knowing weeks of tests would interfere with a busy work schedule, family vacations, etc.

After the initial mammogram, I was called back for a diagnostic version followed by an ultrasound. From there, a biopsy was scheduled the following day. I could see the look on the tech's faces, so when I received a call in less than forty-eight hours that I indeed had cancer—it was really not a shock. I kept the news to myself for a few hours then reached out to a few trusted friends and family members. I had walked the cancer journey alongside several friends over the years, so I knew the battle ahead.

What actions did you take the next several days after?

I got the "cancer call" at 4PM on a Friday, my usual day off to rest and relax. One of my favorite things to do is sit quietly by a fire, so that was my first response to help gather my thoughts. Prayer was and is a huge part of my journey. The first night I tried to be as quiet as possible, talking and listening to the Lord.

I've been an event planner for over twenty years, so my mind automatically shifted to creating a game plan. How do I "outsmart" cancer and go headfirst into the battle without collateral damage; how do I overcome? What I didn't realize at that point—it was too early to devise a game plan. There were several tests and doctors' appointments ahead that would need to take place in order to come up with a plan, and I was trying to fruitlessly rush the system.

Thankfully, I had several mature mentors in my life that kept me from spinning out of control. A good friend referred me to a surgeon, within two days of diagnosis, who expeditiously took the reins, scheduling everything needed while asking me to trust her expertise. Patience and trust were the first lessons in this journey.

WHAT THOUGHTS FLOODED YOUR MIND DURING THE FIRST FEW WEEKS?

The first couple of weeks were filled with tests and scans, so I was busy checking off the boxes. Exactly one month from diagnosis, I had surgery to insert my chemo port, with the first chemo treatment scheduled four days later. From that point the battle was on. The biggest obstacle was the unknown: How would my body react to chemo; would the cancer respond to treatment or spread, would I be able to work, and could I remain active? It was overwhelming.

I had my first chemo on Tuesday, December 7th, and I was determined to try to live as normally as possible. The following, day I was at Orange Theory at 5AM biking ten miles, then to work as normal, followed by a Wednesday evening church service. I was tired, but determined, and the unknown fear was making me even more focused.

That evening, church went a little long, and there was a heavy rainstorm, so I was leaving work later than normal. Once home, I realized I didn't have my cell phone. My iPad was dead, so it took a while to get enough charge to locate my phone. I searched the house, and my car to no avail. I had left my cell at church. Mad at myself for being so careless, I made the trip back to church to find it. I was the only person in the building, even the cleaning crew was gone for the night. I searched my office—no luck—so I determined it must be in the sanctuary. As I searched through the sanctuary, I was praying to find my phone, still angry at myself that I had let my emotions and fear from treatment cause me to be so absent minded. While I was in the sanctuary alone, it was like the Lord had brought me there to be quiet and talk to Him. He had my undivided attention in a sanctuary that seats thousands, where I am always busy. It was just me and Him.

The emotions and tears poured out. Why am I in this battle? I'm healthy, strong, and have served the Lord working for a church over twenty years. How could this be my journey—I'm the one that takes care of everyone else when they are in a battle! That night, I felt He was telling me clearly to live this out well! The Lord was with me, but I was called to fight this battle publicly. I would live this fight out in a way that shows He is with me. To be strong and courageous!

WHAT ADVICE/INFORMATION WOULD YOU GIVE SOMEONE WITH A SIMILAR SITUATION TO BE AN OVERCOMER?

First off, breathe. When you are blindsided by something well beyond your control, you need to stop and gather your mind, heart, and emotions. As I said earlier, prayer has and is a huge part of my journey. Being quiet before the Lord has been a mainstay—something I strategically schedule into my week.

Surround yourself with others that believe in your healing, that will pray with and for you, and limit the voices that speak any negativity over you. Who you spend your time with, who and what you listen to, and what activities you engage in have a huge impact on your mindset. When in battle, choose wisely, and be fine to be alone when needed. Too many voices and distractions in your life are not beneficial, especially if they are not aligned with your goal of overcoming.

I developed a "board of directors," a small core group to help guide me through medical decisions, allowing them the freedom to speak freely into my life as needed.

Lastly, I would say to "find your fight!" I've always been athletic and have competed from a young age, and a cancer diagnosis reminded me of being down in the third set of a singles tennis match. You are on the court alone and can't rely on a teammate to pull you out of trouble; there's no one to blame for mistakes or indecision, and it's up to you to dig deep and fight—to not only stay in the match, but to win! When you are tired, it's easy to become overwhelmed. Be aware of your energy limitations. Set boundaries for yourself to manage your emotions and maintain your strength.

WHAT IS YOUR LONG-TERM PLAN FOR YOUR LIFE?

Great question! I feel like the Lord was very clear with me, live this out well! That has been my goal throughout treatment, and now moving towards life after treatment. I had a total of six heavy chemo sessions, followed by a double mastectomy, and then I returned for another twelve rounds of a targeted treatment. So, the battle has been intense for the past fifteen months. Now it's up to me to live a healthy life, recover, rebuild, and gain strength.

This battle has made me stronger and more aware that we have no guarantees on the longevity or quality of life. As I move forward, I'm trying to find the balance between being productive and also enjoying my time with family and friends, attempting to experience life as much as I can.

I have consciously decided that this diagnosis is only a chapter in my story—it does not define me, and it is not my identity.

Chapter 6

ENOUGH IS ENOUGH!

When you stay ready … you don't have to get ready!

We all have unfinished business. A bad diagnosis or tragic news can zap your energy and threatens to create even more unfinished business. This is a great place for the enemy to knock you off the path.

You must understand that you may have come into this book operating at 70 percent, but you will leave with the how and why to go to 120 percent.

I'm going to help you operate in a way you've never operated before. So, today you can take your life and those with whom you have influence lives to a new and higher level.

How, you might ask? Think more! We are losing or have already lost our ability to T-H-I-N-K.

Your thoughts become your future! No thoughts or negative thoughts make for a lousy future and present. So, stay away from negative people and negative thoughts.

We all have a divine appointment in the future. At this appointment we will be asked, "What did you do with your life "under the sun?" You'll recall, believers, that I believe we live in two times zones: "Time under the SUN" and "Eternity under the SON."

So, write down that one thing that you must get done this year. Enough is enough. You are sick and tired of being sick and tired. *Now* is the time to finally get it done. No task is too big. The bigger the better. Maybe it's a dream you had years ago and you have thought now it's too late. You've set it aside and forgot about it. This is what I'm talking about. Write it down!

Please never confuse knowing with doing. They are two separate things altogether. The message in the book will step on toes for some of us because we know it's true, we need to take more action, and we needed to hear it. If this touches a nerve for you, please pay attention and make entries in your journal. Take some action!

While we all agree to become more successful, it's absolutely essential to continually learn and grow. However, all the knowledge in the world means nothing if you don't take action on it.

"I do not understand what I do. For what I want to do I do not do, but what I hate I do. And if I do what I do not want to do, I agree that the law is good. As it is, it is no longer I, myself, who does it, but it is sin living in me. For I know that good itself does not dwell in me, that is, in my sinful nature. For I have the desire to do what is good, but I cannot carry it out. For I do not do the good I want to do, but the evil I do not want to do—this I keep on doing. Now if I do what I do not want to do, it is no longer I who does it, but it is sin living in me that does it." Romans 7:15-20 (NIV)

We are living in a spiritual conflict between good and evil, seen and unseen. Don't let evil win!

When Good Steps Back ... Evil Sneaks In

I want you to write that one, must-do thing you will finish within the next year. So, next to it write down the year you will accomplish this "must-do" thing. Now, write down the month and day it will be completed. The clock is ticking.

In June of 2023, I had decided that enough is enough! So, I did a video for one of my speaking events where I finally revealed my three-year battle with Parkinson's disease and introduced my new book I was working on titled, *Becoming an Overcomer by Defeating Your Enemies!* This video reached thousands of people. Now, I must confess I was working on this new book, but little was in the form of a manuscript, it was mostly in my head. Then the requests and questions began, "When can we order the book? When will the book be available? Will you have a book signing? When? When? When?"

And that is when I reached my, "Enough is enough!" My commitment to finish for sale and book signing became real and confirmed for December 15th. I booked the space and paid the deposit at the Embassy Suites from 9-1PM. I ordered the refreshments—coffee and hot tea—and booked the photographer, videographer, and people to sell the new book.

Then came the negative professionals, experts on why things can't be done and what could go wrong. I heard, "To soon," "Too busy," and, "Impossible."

My response to the pushback was as per my usual, "I can. I will. I must!" Quitting was not an option.

Remember: Matthew 19:26 says, "Jesus looked at them and said, 'With man this is impossible, but with God all things are possible.'" (NIV) I believe God is in this book and expects me to get it done through His strength. "I CAN—I WILL—I MUST!"

Now write down the name of someone you love and how their life will be changed when you finish the one big thing. Then tell them your "must-do" goal.

Now share your goal with people you know will hold you accountable.

"Procrastination Always Makes Easy Things Hard and Hard Things Harder. What's Easy to Do Is Also Easy Not to Do!"

Procrastination is not real. You just haven't found the thing that's most important to you. What if there was a gun pointed at someone you love and if you don't get the thing accomplished by the deadline your loved one is gone? I bet you won't be playing video games, playing the victim, or watching TV. You won't be playing on social media, partying, sleeping, or shopping on Amazon.

Your Reason Must Be Bigger Than Your Excuses

I signed up for a fifty-mile race. I knew my family would come and watch me, but I never dreamed so many friends would spend a Saturday watching me run fifty miles. But show up they did, young and old, kids, small group members, church friends, neighbors, running club friends, and loads of friends who follow me on social media.

There were many times during the race when I wanted to quit. But thinking of all the people who sacrificed their day to encourage me and who were waiting for me at the finish line made me keep going. They were the reason that was bigger than my excuses.

My family met me in Nashville at the thirty-four mile marker to encourage me and to bring me fresh clothes and shoes and something to eat. I changed clothes and shoes and left them my phone and fuel belt. I knew I wouldn't need that stuff with only sixteen miles to the finish.

So, off I went to the next check-in at mile thirty-five, where I was asked, "Where is your race bib number?" Shocked, I realized it was on my other shirt and I had no way to get it. The checkpoint folks said I could wait till they could talk with the race director (meanwhile, I was losing my current third place race position) or run ahead and be disqualified from the race. Fifty-four minutes later, the race director said let me run to the next checkpoint and they would have me a number. My body was stiff, I had lost many positions, and I wanted to quit, but I remembered all those people waiting for me at the finish. So, I started running again. I had a reason bigger than excuses.

I was struggling around mile thirty-nine and I saw a young runner with a smooth stride running effortlessly ahead of me. So, I slipped in behind him and ran his pace and just let my mind relax and just ran. After about three or four miles the young racer slowed up for me to come along his side which I did. He asked me a question that shocked my world: "Are we going the right way?"

"Going the right way? Are you kidding me? You don't know?" I shouted.

He said he hadn't seen any directional signs in a while. So, we turned back and after about three miles we saw a sign we missed earlier. That means we ran six miles off course. "Just great, six extra miles, thanks a lot!" I yelled and took off in the right direction, leaving the young racer behind.

I really just wanted to quit, and I wanted the day to be over. I got about a half-mile ahead and I heard in my spirit, "It's all your fault. The young racer didn't ask me to run behind him with my mind shut down. My family didn't ask for me to leave my number. Stop playing the victim and take responsibility for your actions."

It's not about what happens to you, but how you respond. I thought again of all the friends and family waiting for me still at the finish line. So, I ran back to the young guy and apologized and we shook hands. I found out his name and where he was from and who he had waiting for him at the finish line. Then I turned and began the final stretch. I just focused and repeated to myself, "I can, I will, I must keep going."

At the finish I couldn't believe the sense of gratitude and accomplishment that overwhelmed me. With man things seem, and many times are, impossible. But with God, all things are possible. Don't quit, don't ring the bell.

"Knowing" is one thing. "Doing" is what makes things happen. Doing is what puts knowledge into motion. Doing is what makes your goals a reality. Doing is the benefit of knowing. Doing is what allows you to live a successful, fulfilled, abundant life. **Never confuse "knowing" for "doing."** You must implement what you've learned to make it valuable and to really benefit from it.

Chapter 7

MIKE AND MONICA HARRIS'S OVERCOMERS STORY

We are Michael and Monica Harris. We were married in 2007. I (Mike) had two children from a previous marriage and Monica had a four-year-old son named Omar. Late in 2016, I started the adoption process with Omar. This was finalized on February 1st of 2017. Also, in this process Omar wanted to change his name. He took the name of Joshua Michael Harris. 2017 was a great year. We were paying off bills. We took our first family vacation. The highlight of the year was Joshua getting baptized in July. We were having a great year and life was good until Sunday, December 3rd. On this day, without warnings or signs or symptoms, Joshua decided to leave this life.

What was your immediate response to your diagnosis or bad news?

Our response was sorrow, shock, disbelief, and pain. We thought, *Could this be real? This can't have happened. Are we dreaming?* We were full of questions. Immediately, our lives were filled with disappointment and despair. Monica had a verse come to her mind during this time. Isiah 55: 8-9. We also found this verse later that perfectly describes how we felt, Jeremiah 6:26: "O daughter of my people, put on sackcloth and roll in ashes; make mourning as for an only son, most bitter lamentation; for suddenly the destroyer will come upon us." (ESV)

Something had happened that we had absolutely no control of and could never change.

WHAT ACTIONS DID YOU TAKE THE NEXT SEVERAL DAYS AFTER?

Our family and friends were a great help during this time. They tried to help us as best as they knew how. These were the hardest days of our lives. Making funeral preparations is never easy, but doing it for your son is devastating. We were lost. We needed help. One of our friends had asked a pastor and his wife to come visit us. Thank The Lord they did. They helped by answering many questions that we had. Where is Joshua now? Why did The Lord allow this to happen? What do we do now? Who can heal our broken heart and spirit?

Wednesday, we had Josh's memorial. We didn't know it but that was the beginning of our healing process. Talking with all Josh's friends and hearing stories about Josh helped us both.

Thursday, we buried our son. One of the hardest days of our lives. Some of our family was spending the night with us so we wouldn't be alone. We were doing all we knew how to get by.

WHAT THOUGHTS FLOODED YOUR MIND DURING THE FIRST FEW WEEKS?

For both of us, probably the thing that kept coming up was wondering what we did wrong. We can remember all the things we said or did wrong. Guilt was a big obstacle. We were both hurting but we knew we didn't want to keep feeling this way. One question that we both had was, "How do we get past so much hurt?" Monica was overcome with anxiety. She couldn't leave the house for more than twenty or thirty minutes at a time. Depression was a reality. It was a very dark time. We felt like we wanted to go to sleep and wake up ten years later. Maybe the pain would be gone.

WHAT ADVICE OR INFORMATION WOULD YOU GIVE SOMEONE WITH A SIMILAR SITUATION?

The thing that we did was to turn to the Lord with all our heart. We prayed and studied our Bible all day every day for a month after the funeral. We invited the Holy Spirit to come into our lives and minister to us. We also prayed in the Spirit every day. When we came to the end of our thoughts, we would pray this way, like making a decision to forgive all people for all things. We also asked for forgiveness for all the wrongs that we had done. We also confessed and asked forgiveness from each other for the things we had done to each other. We tried to remove all barriers between ourselves and God.

We would advise parents to pray daily for their children. They need our help and the help of something more powerful than we are: God.

We surrounded ourselves with Godly people. We changed the places we went and the things we did. We looked for Godly people to mentor us.

We tried to take this attitude towards life: "For whoever does the will of my Father in heaven is my brother, my sister, and my mother." Matthew 12:50 (NIV).

We also started fasting during this time and proclaiming God's Word out loud. All these things we did and are still doing daily. We also looked for places to serve in our local church. Psalm 100: 1-5 is all about praise. We learned to be thankful and praise God in all things.

When Monica felt discouraged, she would read these verses: "Therefore, seeing we are also surrounded by so great cloud of witnesses let us lay aside every weight and the sun that so easily ensures us and let us run with endurance the race that is set before us looking unto Jesus the author and finisher of our faith." Hebrews 12:1-2

WHAT IS YOUR LONG-TERM PLAN FOR YOUR LIFE?

Philippians 3:13-14 has been made our life goal verse. To press on toward the things of God, not letting what has happened in the past weigh or slow us down. We want to serve God with all our heart. To always be used by God for good works that He has for us to do here in this world. To be filled with the wisdom of God and continue to accomplish His task for us in this world. To serve Jesus as His ambassadors here.

In conclusion; Jesus is the answer to all life's problems. By trusting Him and studying the scriptures He will lead you into all truth. Truth for every situation that life has for men. Take up your cross and follow him.

CHAPTER 8

CATCHING YOUR SECOND WIND!

"Enoch walked with God …" Genesis 5:24 (ESV)

Getting in pace with God is painful work, and it's even harder to keep in step with Him because His stride is swift and purposeful and it wears you down. But if you keep going you get your "second wind." To be an overcomer you have to keep going and keep up with God.

The second wind is a phenomenon in long-distance running—like a marathon or an ultra-marathon—when an exhausted runner who appears unable to continue suddenly finds a renewed strength to continue at top performance with less exertion.

Life is harder than we would like it to be. Bad things come when you least expect them. A few years ago, one of my real estate agents was going to list a beautiful, high-end home. She had prepped for a week to ensure she got the listing. Late in the afternoon I saw her and asked, "How did the listing go this morning?"

"I never had the appointment," she said. "On the way there I got a flat tire. It couldn't have happened at a worse time!"

I asked her a question: "When would be a good time for a flat tire?" Open your calendar and let's check the best time for a flat tire, an accident, or a traffic jam.

I've learned it's not what happens to you that matters, it's how you respond that makes the difference in your life conditions. There is never a good time for a bad diagnosis or tragic news. How you respond to it determines whether you will be overcome or be an overcomer. She could have called another agent to give her a ride. She could have called me, and I would have gone with her to the listing appointment, and we would have gotten the listing, I'm sure. She could have called an Uber. Do whatever it takes. You make your choices, then your choices make you. It requires us to think.

I enjoyed endurance running and races for many years. Learning how to transition from running a 10K distance to the half marathon struck me as a natural progression, but not an easy one.

Naturally, as my distance grew, my pace slowed. Slower pace meant slower finishes, which didn't fit well with me, a young military warrior. I felt compelled to pick up the pace and finish in a better position every race.

The same held true going from half marathons to full marathons and then on to the ultra-distance. While training for a half marathon (13.1 miles), I made a decision one afternoon to run at my 10K (6.2 miles) pace. Around my sixth mile, I began running on empty. My lungs burned, my back hurt and my legs were spent. I didn't see any way I could finish the race. I told myself to just run to the next aid station and quit. When I reached the table at the aid station, I grabbed a cup of water and a banana and told myself that once they were gone, I would quit.

When you think you have to quit, don't. Just adjust. Slow down, think positive thoughts, and keep moving forward with baby steps till you get some momentum.

Surprisingly, once I'd finished the water and eaten the banana, I found myself still running—slower than I wanted but advancing. Then something happened. My breathing became less labored, my legs stopped aching, and my mind cleared. I had a second wind. My body gave up and my mind took over! Mind over matter!

You see, you are always six inches, "this close," to a breakthrough or to failure because you are "this close," six inches. The six inches between your ears is your mind and it is a battlefield. What you think about, you bring about. Keep thinking you can't go on and you won't. Keep thinking, "I can, I will, I must," keep going and you will. The pain will eventually stop, but quitting lasts forever. You are an overcomer.

LIFE IS NOT A SPECTATOR SPORT!

I began to run faster with less effort and felt like I could run all day. I can't explain a second wind, but I know it's real. The same is true in life and business when we find ourselves trying to stay in step with an ever-changing world.

Seemingly the world just keeps spinning around faster and faster until we want to get off, or until we're just hanging on for dear life. Life comes at us fast and full of challenges and bad news. There is no "pause" button. We have to get back on pace or be left behind. Again, be overcome or be an overcomer. It's a binary decision no one should make for you.

Technology advances faster than ever before and artificial intelligence is growing at a record pace. We are constantly connected, using up a chunk of our 1,440 daily minutes. Be more concerned about how you are spending your days and life than spending your money. It matters more in time and eternity!

Life Out of Balance Is an Unbalanced Life

The world is changing, and we are changing with it. We find ourselves eating faster, walking faster, and talking faster than we used to. Without knowing how or why it is so, there is always more to do and less time in which to get it done.

We fill and then overfill our days. Applications for our smart devices have changed us culturally and socially. Keeping pace is difficult. Now throw a bad diagnosis or tragic news in the mix. Too many times we quit or give up before we get our second wind. Never quit. Never give up. Keep advancing.

Again, I have no idea how a second wind works. I just know second winds happen 100 percent of the time if we hang in there long enough for it to kick in. Since we don't know exactly when the second wind will kick into place, we must stay the course until it does. God is able and faithful.

Before You Get Your Second Wind in Life, There's a Little Bit of Panic, Anxiety, Stress, and a Sense of Doom and Discomfort.

The second wind works in every area of your life. I've seen it work in the personal, the financial, and the spiritual. The second wind has worked for me, so I know it will work for you! No matter what your current circumstances, it's never too late to pursue that second wind—a force that will propel you forward into God's best for your life. I don't know what is going on in your life right now, but I can tell you to hang on, keep going, and don't stop because your "second wind" is coming. Too many times, we give up before we receive the second wind.

What age are you? You might think, "I'm past the age of doing any of this stuff. My time has passed."

When I turned fifty, a friend told me, "It's all downhill from here; you are now officially over the hill."

My response, "Not if I find another hill to climb."

In my fifties, that's exactly what I did. I trained and ran a fifty-mile race, I began a speaking career, I became an author, and I set a few personal-best sales years in real estate. I rode my motorcycle from Murfreesboro, Tennessee to Key West, Florida and went deep sea fishing. I found my second wind and so can you. Keep going. Keep the pace.

Realize that it's never over until it's over. Understand that, no matter how old or set in your ways you are, God never intends for your life to be locked in. He always has more for you to experience and learn, as long as you're alive.

Invite and expect Him to surprise you with His creative ideas for new directions you can take in life. Don't rule out anything—a career change, a move, etc. Remember, we must invest our time concerned about His plan and purpose and not our relief. He has a plan. Seek Him first and the rest will be added to you.

HERE ARE FIVE WAYS TO GET YOUR SECOND WIND IN LIFE:

1. **Know your why: Your reason must be bigger than your excuses.** If we are running and we start to walk, then walking becomes easier later on.

   If quitting is an option, then we take it. Quitting then becomes easier later on. If we know our why, then we can come up with the "how to." It begins each day with a check-in with ourselves.

   What's your goal? What's your purpose? Who are you connecting with? Identify two must-do priorities for the day before you walk out the door. Stay focused on them.

2. **Don't stop.** When I coached, one of my athletes was going to break two hours for a half marathon. I was running with her, pacing her. It was going to be close! On the very last slight up-hill, 300 yards from the finish, she stopped! I screamed at her to get going! She finished in 1:59:52.

   No matter how bad something hurts in our life, there is an endpoint. Everything on Earth has an expiration date except your Spirit. The pain period we are going through will stop! Quitting lasts forever.

   Hard times do not come to stay, they come to pass. *If* you *stop*, then all bets are off. You have to keep moving to get your second wind.

3. **Find your rhythm.** Everything has a rhythm. Life has momentum. In the courtroom, the best defense is to "object." It gets the other lawyer off their rhythm! Tennis players go back to their towel. Baseball hitters step in and out of the batter's box—all in an attempt to get the opponent off their rhythm.

   Find your rhythm, breath, and get back to your routine. Breath, reset, re-focus, get back to your routine. Oh, yes, and breathe.

4. **Have patience.** We want our second wind in life ***now***. We just don't know when it will come. We can't know. All that is certain is that if we go through the motions, if we check-out, if we start looking for the exit, then, our next wind won't happen!

   I had someone once tell me, **"I can't wait to be patient."** Patience a higher-order skill and one in which we do not practice today. I can guarantee you that your second wind in life is coming if you just hang on long enough.

5. **Know what moves the needle in your life.** Know the "vital few" things that generate the majority of your

success in life. Practice these things the most and reduce the "busy" work. Outsource, limit, or delete the busy work from your life.

"Do you not know that in a race all the runners run, but only one gets the prize? Run in such a way as to get the prize" 1 Corinthians 9:24 (NIV)

You should place more value on the struggles you have endured in life than the successes you have enjoyed.

Where in your life have you struggled to keep up? What's one area where you need to speed up your pace and get in stride? Where are you falling behind and running at a slower pace? Pick one and don't give up because the second wind is coming. You are an overcomer.

We don't know when or we don't know how, we just know the second wind is coming. Once you get that second wind, things will become easier and more successful than ever before. You will also become more confident in your ability to hang on because the second wind is coming!

Chapter 9

LIVING A "FRET-FREE" LIFE

"Do not fret because of those who are evil or be envious of those who do wrong; for like the grass they will soon wither, like green plants they will soon die away." Psalm 37:1-2 (NIV)

Stop comparing your life to others you know or to those on *Fakebook*! You are an overcomer. Claim it! Fretting means getting ourselves "out of joint" mentally or spiritually because of a bad diagnosis or tragic news.

It's easy to say, "Rest in the Lord, and wait patiently for Him," (Psalm 37:7, KJV) until our own little world is turned upside down and seems we are forced to live in confusion, loss, trauma, and agony like many other people.

When we look around, we see the world full of evildoers, that appear to flourish and live in ease. We are tempted to *fret* at this, to think of them as happy people, and so we are tempted to do like them; But this we are warned against.

Outward prosperity is fading. When we look forward with an eye of faith, we see no reason to envy the wicked or the lawless. Their weeping and wailing will be everlasting.

The life of a Christ follower is a believing trust in the Lord, and diligent care to serve Him according to His will in all circumstances. It is not trusting God, but tempting Him, if we don't trust and obey, which is our duty to Him. He knows what is best for His plan and us.

To delight in God is as much a privilege as a duty. He has not promised to gratify the appetites of the body, but the desires of the renewed, sanctified soul. What is the desire of the heart of a Christ follower? It is to know, love, and serve God. Commit your way unto the Lord even under the most difficult times. You will become an overcomer.

Cast your burden upon the Lord. We must roll (this fretting) off ourselves, not afflict and perplex ourselves with thoughts about future events, what-ifs, and envy, but give them to God.

To stop fretting means getting away from attacks on us mentally or spiritually. It is one thing to say, "Fret not," but a very different thing to have such a disposition that you find yourself able not to fret. (The *mind* is a battlefield. It's where the fretting begins.)

It sounds so easy to talk about resting in the Lord and waiting patiently for him until your nest is upset—until we live, as so many are doing, amidst challenge, whether with financial or health problems and anguish. Is it possible then to rest in the Lord?

If this "don't" does not work there, it will work nowhere. This "don't" must work in days of perplexity as well as in days of peace, or it never will work. And if it will not work in your particular case, it will not work in anyone else's case. Resting in the Lord does not depend on external circumstances at all, but on your relationship to God Himself, especially in troubled times. He is your refuge.

Keep in Mind:

1. **Fretting always ends in sin.** We imagine that a little anxiety and worry are an indication of how really wise we are;

it is much more an indication of how really wicked we are. We must trust God in every situation good or tragic.

2. **Fretting comes from a determination to get our own way.** Our Lord never worried and He was never anxious, because He was not "out" to realize His own plan. He was "out" to realize God's plan.
3. **Fretting is wicked if you are a child of God.** Have you been bolstering up that soul of yours with the idea that your circumstances are too much for God? Put all "what-ifs" on one side and dwell in the shadow of the Almighty. Deliberately tell God that you will not fret about anything. All our fret and worry are caused by our planning without God.

TO COMBAT WORRY, TRY THIS:

1. **Don't plan without God.** God seems to have a special way of upsetting the plans we have made, when we have made them without considering Him. We get ourselves into circumstances that were not chosen by God, and suddenly we realize that we have been making our plans without Him— that we have not even considered Him to be a factor in the planning of our lives. And yet, the only thing that will keep us from even the possibility of worrying is to bring God in as the greatest factor in all of our planning especially in dire situations. Only through God can we become an overcomer.

In spiritual issues it is customary for us to put God first, but we tend to think that it is inappropriate and unnecessary to put him first in the practical, everyday issues of our lives. If we have the idea that we have to put on our "perfect spiritual face" before we can come near to God, then we will never come near to Him. We must come as we are. Be real and authentic.

2. **Don't plan with a concern for evil in mind.** Does God really mean for us to plan without taking the evil around us into account? "Love … thinks no evil." 1 Corinthians 13:4-5 Love is not ignorant of the existence of evil, but it does not take it into account as a factor in planning.

   When we were apart from God, we did take evil into account, doing all of our planning with it in mind, and we tried to reason out all of our work from its standpoint. Do you have a plan for the future? How do you make your plans? Process? We fight the enemy, Satan, under the strength of God not our own.
3. **Don't plan with a rainy day in mind.** You cannot hoard things for a rainy day if you are truly trusting Christ. Jesus said, "Let not your heart be troubled…" (John 14:1). God will not keep your heart from being troubled. Rather, this is a command, "*Let not …*" To do it, continually pick yourself up, even if you fall a hundred and one times a day, until you get into the habit of putting God first and planning with Him in mind. No more being a victim, and no more pity party. You are a child of God, and you are an overcomer.

To be an unshakeable follower of Jesus, we must have courage, endurance, perseverance, and *trust* God in all circumstances!

Prayer: Heavenly Father, my desire is to be pleasing in your sight. I want to be an overcomer. You have given me great blessings, far beyond what I have earned or deserved. Lord, I ask you to remove fretting from my life so that I might focus on serving you. Help me to gain a Kingdom perspective. Give me wisdom that I might serve you well all the days of my life. I choose to yield to your truth to give me the strength, endurance, and courage to follow you. Holy Spirit, help me to honor my Lord and my God. In Jesus's name, amen.

CHAPTER 10

RANDY AND LESLIE DICKERSON'S OVERCOMERS STORY

I describe myself as a focused individual. I own a very busy business. I have a family that depends on me heavily. I have always handled tragedy well because actions after the fact cannot change the situation. My main outlet is to be productive in all endeavors. I am determined to stay busy. Idle times have led to bad decisions for me in the past.

WHAT WAS YOUR IMMEDIATE RESPONSE TO YOUR BAD NEWS?

Our bad news came twice, four years apart. We lost our oldest son, Eric, and four years later we lost our second son, Josh. The first time I was notified that his body had been found and I was asked to come to identify it. I recall a thirty-minute drive filled with anxiety, mostly because I realized that I was the patriarch of the family. The anxiety was initially surrounding the thought of, *How will my wife receive this?* Obviously, sorrow and disappointment overcame all feelings.

Being the elder, I had a wife, sons, and a granddaughter to be mindful about. I had to be strong since I would be depended on to lead through this tragedy. I decided that I must guard my deepest sorrow until more appropriate times. In the times I was alone I would allow myself to grieve and reflect.

The second time, I was first to find Josh's lifeless body. A 911 call operator talked me through administering CPR. Therefore, I wouldn't accept that he was gone. During an hour or so wait at the emergency room I came to accept that he was gone. A couple of close friends arrived to be by my side, thankfully, very Godly ones. I couldn't understand how God could let this happen again to us. We had prayed so fervently for these young men. Before leaving the hospital, my wife had notified our family and I again became the patriarch leader, saving my grief for my personal times.

WHAT ACTIONS DID YOU TAKE THE SEVERAL DAYS AFTER?

Both times, the first days went by without much rest and sleep. We were, each time, for two or three days in a state of shock. The phone calls, texts, emails, visits, and prayers from our caring family, friends, and most importantly, our church family, really strengthened us. The business parts kept us busy and focused for several days. Only after the funerals did the realization of the events truly become totally realistic. Probably the month after the funerals were the hardest because most of the well-wishing dwindled. But the close church family and relatives checking in and praying us through this period. To this day, four to eight years later, thoughts, prayers and remembrances are very helpful.

WHAT THOUGHTS FLOODED YOUR MINDS THOSE FIRST FEW WEEKS?

Each son had a young daughter. The older one had a wife who was not in the picture. Therefore, we have adopted that young girl. The second son had a daughter who wanted to spend all of her time with him. The ex-wife would gain full custody. My thoughts became primarily about those little girls growing up without a father. How could I (Randy) fulfill their needs? Also, the question of God allowing this was constantly in my thoughts. I frequently wondered if we would overcome these losses and not allow them to change our attitude, faith, and emotions.

WHAT ADVICE WOULD YOU GIVE SOMEONE WITH A SIMILAR SITUATION TO BE AN OVERCOMER?

Over the following weeks, in each case, fellow believers would tell us of circumstances, dreams, words from God and other things that confirmed our sons were in the presence of Jesus. One of the pastors from the first funeral advised us to pray for confirmation. The prayers were answered abundantly. I came to realize that our sons had achieved what we are striving for, that is, to see Jesus. My pastor said in the first funeral that God knows how to get His people to home.

After the second death, this pastor was gracious to sit down and discuss the enormous weight I had with grieving families and two little girls, to raise one and be there as father/grandfather to the other, as well as difficult economic impact. The list was long and heavy. He told me, for he knew the family's history well, that I had a big plateful, but I had to eat it one bite at a time and not all at one time. I follow this advice daily.

So, my advice is to trust God's way and be a part of a group of Bible believing people to support, pray, and fellowship to build strength. Believe and trust in God's promises.

WHAT IS YOUR LONG-TERM PLAN FOR YOUR LIFE?

I plan to continue seeking God and to try to be closer each day to him. I plan to teach my surviving son, granddaughters, employees, and all who trust in me to seek God first. I intend to give Him the credit for seeing us through. I intend to be strong and stronger and rest in the fact that I will rejoice with those young men in the presence of Jesus when I see Him. I see people who grieve endlessly and think, *This cannot be good for their health and strength.* Yes, we have to grieve, but we cannot weaken ourselves in that. My wife received words from the Holy Spirit to reflect on the time with them because not everyone has had the opportunity to know those they lost.

Chapter 11

A LIFE WITHOUT LIMIT!

"Our Lives Are Always Moving in the Direction of Our Strongest Thoughts."

The life we have is a reflection of what we think. Our mind is capable of more than we know. In ten years, we will each look in the mirror and someone will stare back. That person will be shaped by the thoughts of today.

Your beliefs have a lot to do with what your reality becomes. If you believe your chance for a happy life again is impossible, you're probably right. If you believe you can do all things through Him who gives you strength, you will be an overcomer.

"One day as Jesus was standing by the Lake of Gennesaret, the people were crowding around him and listening to the word of God. He saw at the water's edge two boats, left there by the fishermen, who were washing their nets. He got into one of the boats, the one belonging to Simon, and asked him to put out a little from shore. Then he sat down and taught the people from the boat.

"When he had finished speaking, he said to Simon, 'Put out into deep water, and let down the nets for a catch.'

"Simon answered, 'Master, we've worked hard all night and haven't caught anything. But because you say so, I will let down the nets.'"

"When they had done so, they caught such a large number of fish that their nets began to break." Luke 5:1-6 (NIV)

You see, that the disciples were "washing their nets" was a sign they were finished for the day. They were tired and disappointed because they caught no fish all night. They were ready to quit, but God had bigger plans.

So many times, we stay near the shore—near our comfortable zone. But notice that God had the disciples put out their nets into the deep water. In order to do *big* things, we need to get out into the deep water. Stop living in the shallow water of your life.

With God ALL things are possible.

"Feed What's Feeding You!"

It's important to examine your beliefs because you live your life based upon your beliefs and nothing else. What you believe you will achieve. The size of your success is determined by the size of your belief.

Henry Ford shared: "Whether you think you can, or think you can't, you're right." The ability to achieve your highest aspirations depends on two things: belief and action. To see a permanent change on the outside, you must first create the change of belief on the inside. Your life always moves in the direction of your beliefs. What you believe matters. You are responsible for your life. Believe that this bad news will change into a blessing as long as you don't quit.

Where are you playing the victim instead of taking responsibility for your life? Failure is not a disastrous end but a steppingstone to success. Sometimes, things fall apart so better things can fall together. Though you may see no way out of your current situation remember that no matter how good or bad your situation is, it will change. Don't get comfortable.

The only thing you can truly control is yourself. The more you concentrate on what you can control—your own preparation and responses—the better you can adapt to whatever situation you find yourself in. Never succumb to the pressures of Satan and his tactics to overcome you. Keep progressing as you defeat the enemy and become an overcomer.

Your Income Will Rarely Exceed Your Level of Personal and Professional Development. Your Best Chance of Getting Everything You Want and Need Is—You!

Life is messy and chaotic. But we can be thankful that our paths aren't straight. Embrace the chance to spend some time on the backroads. Often, the best things in life are the ones we discover on the detours. God has you on a path, keep going. You don't know what the future holds, but you know who holds the future. You can trust Him each day. The best time to do something is when you don't have to.

Everything Will Be Okay in the End—If It's Not Okay, It's not the End!

You already have everything you need to get started. Getting started is perhaps the biggest obstacle in life. A few, simple changes in beliefs can make all the difference. Consider the impact your beliefs are having on your life and finetune any beliefs that limit your potential for a more successful, fulfilling life for you and all with whom you have influence. You are an overcomer!

CHAPTER 12

CHAD MOLITOR'S OVERCOMER STORY: MUSCLE INVASIVE BLADDER CANCER

I would say that I've always had a passion for life and "seizing the day." I have always hoped for my family and I to live our best life (in relationships, ministry, traveling, business success, enjoyable hobbies, etc.). God has blessed me abundantly throughout my life, including with my wife of thirty-five years, my children and grandchildren, my thriving investment advisory career, my wonderful church, my deep-rooted friendships, and by allowing me to serve on the boards of two wonderful ministries. Not to mention, I've had the ability to explore hobbies and pursuits that I'm passionate about. No one's life is ever perfect of course, but I was in a great place. So, the cancer diagnosis I received in 2022 was completely out of left field and my family and I were rather stunned.

WHAT WAS YOUR IMMEDIATE RESPONSE TO YOUR HEALTH DIAGNOSIS OR BAD NEWS?

I don't think the reality of a tumor took hold in my heart and mind at first, perhaps from denial (I have been "crunchy" since before crunchy was cool and I'm the last person I thought would ever hear the three words, "You have cancer"). Or, perhaps it was because I am an optimist. But once I began to accept things, it all started to sink in: fear, worry, questions, and wondering what caused it. *Why me?* I found myself immediately reprioritizing my present and future plans. I knew this illness was going to be a difficult valley to walk through for my family and me.

My mind went to the "lists" that I needed to start checking off, to the things that I felt I still had some control over at a time of much uncertainty. I planned for the research I would do, my work, and how my business would be handled while I took the time needed to fight this battle. Fortunately, I knew my son Parker is very capable of taking over Molitor Wealth Management, our investment advisory business, while I did research and treatments. And my wife (Shelly), two adult children (Parker and Bree), and daughter-in-law (Michelle) were a rock for me from beginning to end of this journey.

WHAT ACTIONS DID YOU TAKE IN THE NEXT SEVERAL DAYS AFTER?

For me it all began when I noticed blood in my urine, and I expected a kidney stone or something of the like. After many scans and doctor visits (by the grace of God I have a wonderful surgeon friend that helped guide me and speed the initial process along) it was discovered that I had a 4.9-centimeter tumor on the inside dome of my bladder. The following days and weeks consisted of various scans, tests, and consultations. After a scope procedure, I was told that my doctor was unable to remove the cancerous tumor because it was what is called MIBC (muscle invasive bladder cancer). He said this meant the bladder must come out before the cancer might grow through the outer muscle layer of the bladder and spread through my body. At this point I also started to hit the research hard, digging deep to find objective information from unbiased sources so that I could (prayerfully) make the best and most informed medical decisions for myself. A cystoprostatectomy with ileal conduit is an invasive surgery, but it turns out chemo was the bigger challenge. Symptoms get progressively worse as chemo builds up in your system. Yes, my hair fell out and I became weaker and more nauseated each month.

My oncologist and the nursing staff were the best, but I dreaded the days I had to go in for chemo treatments. However, on the bright side, I experienced a wonderful outpouring of support when people heard the news about my cancer and rallied around my family and me. Dozens and dozens sent cards, emails, or texts on a regular basis to check in and send me an encouraging scripture passage or a prayer. It was like having my funeral without first having to die to see how many people truly cared. Many different people called or texted to say, not just "I'm praying for you," but, "I'm praying for you and your family every day!" That was certainly a huge blessing during a difficult time.

What Thoughts Flooded Your Mind During the First Few Weeks?

Someone asked me early on if I was going to pray or go see a doctor? And I said, "Yes," meaning, "Both." After the incredibly unexpected cancer diagnosis sunk in, my first hope and prayer was for God to heal me outright, without the need for medical intervention. I had hopes that upon revisiting the doctor he would say, "The cancer was here last week, but somehow, it's gone now! Go home and live your life." But that is not what happened, so my second prayer was for God to guide me in the research to find the best of the best in the medical fields that I would need: oncologists, urologists, surgeons, etc. One of the ways God answered that prayer was through the help of a close friend who had also been through a cancer battle. I also found some objective sources to rate the different hospitals and surgeons who performed a relatively high number of the cystoprostatectomy with ileal conduit surgeries that I needed. Through further research and prayer for discernment, we boiled it down to the twenty best surgeons in the Eastern United States, and then we narrowed it down to the top five. I then interviewed all five of them in person or by Zoom and finally decided upon the number one pick for a surgeon. And my number one pick for the best oncologist happened to be a longtime friend of mine.

A major prayer theme for me at this time was based on Hezekiah in the book of Second Kings, when the prophet Isaiah came to him and said, "Your time on the earth is finished, pack your bags, this is your last day on the earth, you're going to eternity." (living version) But Hezekiah turned toward the lord and prayed earnestly for God to extend his time on the earth. God told him that he had heard his prayers and seen his tears and was going to give him fifteen more years on the earth. This gives me hope that even when our days are numbered and the number comes to an end, God can move on our behalf and extend our time on the earth like he did for Hezekiah.

The second prayer theme that my family and I leaned into is based on Shadrach, Meshach, and Abednego: before they went into the fiery furnace, they said, "We know our God is able to deliver us, but even if He doesn't, for some reason of his own that we don't understand, we still trust him." I still trust him, even if he had some reason not to heal me—that was a tough realization to come to! But that's where the lesson was for me.

Another thought that stuck with me at this time was that all the really "big" people I know in life (large in character and close to God) have been through a significant trial or multiple trials or tests in which they've had to lean on God, and he brought them through it.

Since I was having to endure this pain, fear, and loss, I wanted to squeeze out every last drop of benefit. As James 1:2-4 says, "Count it all joy, my brothers, and sisters, when you meet trials of various kinds, for you know that the testing of your faith produces endurance, spiritual maturity, and inner peace. And let endurance have its perfect result that you may be completely developed, lacking nothing" (ESV). These are the directions I returned to in my thoughts whenever I began to feel overwhelmed with it all.

WHAT ADVICE/INFORMATION WOULD YOU GIVE SOMEONE IN A SIMILAR SITUATION, TO BE AN OVERCOMER?

My pastor and friend of thirty-seven years, Allen Jackson, gave me some great advice that I hung onto throughout the cancer battle. "Begin to thank God now for your healing, even if you can't see how or when it will work out." So that's what I did, and that's what I would advise anyone else in a tough situation to do as well. Prayer is our most important tool. I firmly believe that God moves on our behalf when we come to Him earnestly, much like we come to the aid of our own earthly children when they are in need. It's important to live well through this challenging time because the next generation is watching. It's an opportunity to be an example and a blessing to loved ones. Especially the little people (grandchildren). I would also add that it's important to be a good steward of medical decisions that need to be made, and to spend the time and research that is necessary for you to make the best choices and to be an advocate for yourself when working with your doctors.

WHAT IS YOUR LONG-TERM PLAN FOR YOUR LIFE?

If there's one thing I've learned in my fifty-eight years on earth, it's that life is about relationships. God, spouse, family, friends, business...these integral connections affect every aspect of my life, with faith in God at the center of it all. I have been extremely blessed with a Godly wife of thirty-five years, two wonderful adult children, and three precious grandchildren. My church of thirty-five years has given me dozens more impactful friendships and a deep root of faith and community. It can be easy to go through life taking all these many relationships for granted, and little did I know a year ago just how cherished the support, prayers, and outpouring of love from so many people would become to me. I am very grateful to God for healing me and bringing my family and I through this difficult valley, and the experience certainly changed my life and caused me to reprioritize. It's been a catalyst to stay present and live in the moment. So, my plan is to continue doing just that, striving to live every day in the fullness of relationship with God and others.

CHAPTER 13

LIVING A LIFE OF NO REGRETS

"Regret sneaks in when you fail to live your life as your most authentic self."

Looking in the rearview mirror, I can vividly see areas of my life that I regret, though my regrets are not the usual suspects. I've traveled extensively, jumped out of perfectly good airplanes, completed endurance races, owned companies, and taken great risk with great rewards. I'm blessed to have written books, to have shared at my speaking events, and to have brokered real estate deals every day.

My regrets stem more from not loving enough, not being there for my children when they were very young. Not telling my friends how much I loved them and how much they meant to me. Not hugging enough and not being there for those who needed me the most. I regret every time I told others and myself my excuse—"I was doing it for my family"—when my family would prefer me to be with them.

I was never satisfied and often consumed with myself. I often say most of us could write a book titled, *I Ain't Much, but I'm All I Ever Think About*. Chapter One: Me; Chapter Two:

Me, and so on. Add this to a bad diagnosis of Parkinson's and I was easily, fully consumed with myself. Even though I knew better from my past and I knew my family needed me now more than ever, it took a few minutes to switch off *me* and turn on *them*. Now I am able to think more about others instead of myself. I had to learn this behavior and change on the inside first. That's what it means to be an overcomer.

I've changed during the past decade. I made the effort to put the needs of others before my own. I tell friends how much I love them and value our relationship. I attend basketball games, dance recitals, swim lessons, and tennis and soccer games with my grandchildren. I play hide-and-seek and cards, and I laugh now more than ever.

A 2010 Harvard study revealed that up to 80 percent of Americans have a major regret, or regrets, in their lives. What are your regrets?

I never planned or even imagined that I would have Parkinson's disease at this stage of my life. So many of us put off traveling or some other bucket list items till we retire. We don't know how long we have here under the sun or even what tomorrow will bring. I am glad I have lived life to the fullest I could and have committed to do everything possible to live as much life as possible every day I have left. Keep moving and live in the present. It's all you have.

Without thinking, you could end up going through life on "autopilot." It's easy to be overcome when you are operating on autopilot. You are unaware and unconcerned.

I often asked my audience at my speaking engagements, "Have you ever driven someplace familiar and upon arrival at your destination, not remember the drive? Physically you were there in the vehicle driving, but emotionally and mentally you were somewhere else." That's autopilot. You are running through life with no self-awareness. Now add a bad diagnosis or tragic news and you could easily shut down all together. You will be overcome and just surviving not thriving. This will lead you to regrets in the final chapters of your life.

HERE ARE SOME OF THE TOP REGRETS FOR MOST:

- Not traveling more.
- Not being true to yourself. (Living for others and their expectations.)
- Not learning more (through education, training, and experiences).
- Not spending more time with family and friends.
- Not following your inner voice, your path, your passion. (Fear)
- Not loving others more fully. Not letting them know!

INACTION IS THE MOST DEVASTATING REGRET

Regret is the one wound you can't recover from. You will have memories. What will they be? We can't change the past but we can sure do something about the future.

"Brothers, I do not consider that I have made it my own. But one thing I do: forgetting what lies behind and straining forward to what lies ahead, I press on toward the goal for the prize of the upward call of God in Christ Jesus."
Philippians 3:13 (ESV)

I haven't figured it all out, but now I "live–laugh–love" every day. My priorities are ordered as follows: God first, my wife second, my children and grandkids third, and my country next.

My friends know I love and value them. My wife, Shelly, will say, "Would you like to go to dinner with …" And I'll answer "Yes" before she announces their names. I love people.

When I got Covid and had to be quarantined I thought I would go nuts. I really enjoy being with people. I joke at my events that during my time quarantined I was so desperate I began talking at length with the spam callers from the car warranty companies.

My past doesn't define me, though it has prepared me to live a life with no regrets and so can you.

Each of us would like a "do over" for something in our past. We've all said or done things we wished we hadn't. We can't change what's happened, but we can adjust our sails and head in a new direction. Where do you need an adjustment in your sails? What must you do to reduce the regrets for the future? You are an overcomer!

Chapter 14

LAUNCHING HOLY SPIRIT POWER

"And you shall receive power when the Holy Spirit has come upon you; and you shall be my witnesses in Jerusalem and in all Judea and Samaria and to the end of the earth." Acts 1:8

A child of God needs the enabling power of the Holy Spirit to live victoriously. The power of God is vital for the challenges that we will face, like a bad diagnosis or tragic news. We are not exempt. You cannot become an overcomer without the power and help of the Holy Spirit. This power that Jesus speaks about is not a one-time resource. In fact, the Bible talks about how the disciples repeatedly sought God for refreshing, and so should we. Why? Because we leak and constantly need refilling.

The Holy Spirit plays many roles. You can read about some of them in these passages: John 14:15-27, John 16:5-15, Romans 8:1-17, and Galatians 5:16-26.

In John 14, for example, Jesus says the Holy Spirit will comfort us when we're hurting. "I will not leave you as orphans,"

Jesus says (14:18, ESV), promising that the Spirit will bring us peace (14:27).

Jesus also says the Spirit will help us recall the things we've learned about God (14:26)—which also means the Spirit will help us when we tell others about our faith and how we became overcomers.

I mentioned earlier that in John 16 Jesus refers to the Spirit as a "Counselor" who will guide us in our everyday lives. One way He'll guide us is by convicting us of sin (16:8). God wants us to get rid of the things that displease Him, and the most powerful way to identify those things is to be convicted by the Spirit.

Romans 8 tells us the Spirit will help us stop sinning and do the things that please God, and it also tells us that the Spirit helps us pray (8:26). We've all said to God, "Lord, I'm just not sure how to pray or what to say."

As I've previously mentioned, the Holy Spirit actually intercedes for us, saying the prayers *for* us. Sometimes we find ourselves in a strange and unfamiliar place...uncharted waters. We don't know which way to turn and wonder whether we should just shelter in place?

The Holy Spirit won't do the work for us alone. We must to do our part—especially to consistently read our Bibles and pray, asking the Spirit to show us the truth and teach us how to live and lead us on our path.

It's important to remember that the Spirit will not ask us to do anything that is contrary to Scripture. We need to make sure we're listening to the voice of the Holy Spirit, not the voice of our own selfish desires. And we can verify and distinguish this by checking the voice against the truth of God's Word.

Acts 2:4 says, "And they were filled with the Holy Spirit." (NKJV) And after receiving this power, they came back to

God for a refreshing against the new threats that they were facing.

A little further down, in Acts 4:31, it says, "And when they had prayed, the place in which they were gathered together was shaken and they were all filled with the Holy Spirit, and they spoke the word of God with boldness." (NKJV)

Also consider this selection from Ephesians 3:14–21 (ESV): "For this reason I bow my knees before the Father, from whom every family in heaven and on earth is named, that according to the riches of His glory He may grant you to be strengthened with might through His Spirit in your inner being, so that Christ may dwell in your hearts through faith—that you, being rooted and grounded in love, may have strength to comprehend with all the saints what is the breadth and length and height and depth, and to know the love of Christ which surpasses knowledge, that you may be filled with all the fullness of God.

"Now to Him who by the power at work within us is able to do far more abundantly than all that we ask or think, according to the power at work within us, to him be glory in the church and in Christ Jesus to all generations, forever and ever. Amen."

NOW, WE ALREADY KNOW THAT WE KNOW WE NEED THE POWER OF THE HOLY SPIRIT. LET'S REVISIT THE FIVE WAYS TO RECEIVE IT:

1. **Read (and re-read) the Word of God.** God equips you with His power to enable you to proclaim His Word successfully. It is important to immerse yourselves in His Word, which *is* life itself. This requires us to read His Word daily.

   In John 6:63 Jesus said, "It is the Spirit that gives life, the flesh is of no avail; the words that I have spoken to you are Spirit and life." (NABRE) The Bible, the Word of

God, pours out the life-giving power of the Spirit to those who read it and receive it. Immersed in God's Word, we jumpstart and increase our faith, which helps us walk in the power of the Holy Spirit. We will need more faith and more of the Holy Spirit as time moves forward.

2. **Seek God's face.** We need to seek the face of God and pursue His presence consistently and relentlessly. When we wait on God, we renew the power to walk this life in the Spirit. In all circumstances we need the power of the Holy Spirit, but especially in times of trouble we need it more. The Bible says, "All these with one accord devoted themselves to prayer." Acts 1:13 (RSVCE)

   It can't be overstated: We must also take daily to withdraw from the world and the Weapons of Mass Distraction around us to seek His face. Bible says Jesus came with full of power after his forty days of fasting. Extended fasting and prayer are key to receiving God's power.

   Look, God has given you everything you will need to survive this life under the sun, but it will take everything you got. You will need the power of the Holy Spirit in these most difficult days. Invite the Holy Spirit into your life and plans early and often.

   Those times that we seek God should be a time of surrendering and learning to yield to the plans and purposes of the Holy Spirit. In the midst of our biggest challenges, we must be concerned about God's plans and purposes not our relief.

3. **Believe the promise of God through his Word:** "It is impossible to please God without faith." Hebrews 11:6

   We cannot walk in the power of the Holy Spirit if we do not walk by faith.

   Luke 11:13 Jesus says to his disciples, "If you then, who are evil, know how to give good gifts to your children, how much more will the heavenly Father give the Holy Spirit to those who ask Him!" (ESV) Start by asking today! Ask God to increase your faith. The Lord desires to fill you with His power.

4. **Rest and Recharge in Him.** It is not enough to receive God's power once. Why wouldn't we want to claim the fullness of what God has for us? We need to continue to reside in Him. You need to take time to study the Word and abide in it.

   John 14:12- 23 explains how obeying God and keeping His commandments is essential to having a life filled with God's power.
5. **Love One Another.** "This is my commandment, that you love one another as I have loved you." John 15:12 (NKJV) You recall, Jesus came for the sick. Toward the end of the ministry of Jesus, He took much effort talking to them about loving each other and even showing them service by washing their feet.

So, we must immerse ourselves in His word and put to death every unbelief and commit ourselves to fast and pray for His power to manifest through our lives.

Prayer: Heavenly Father, Thank you for the gift of the Holy Spirit. Help me to not only connect, but also continuously reconnect to the power of the Holy Spirit so I might walk in the steps You order for me. Holy Spirit you are welcome into every area of my life. Help us to guard our hearts so we are not distracted or diminished in our pursuit of God's best for our lives. May the name of Jesus be lifted up, amen.

CHAPTER 15

DESPERATE TIMES!

Sometimes we are in such a difficult place we think there is no way it can get worse. Then it does. With no end in sight, we begin to believe there is no way out. Add to this us thinking under our limited strength and limited experience and we are right—it's hopeless.

Christ followers tend to gauge their levels of victory by comparing themselves to the world's standards rather than the promises of God's Word. Overcomers in the Bible were generally not winners by the world's criteria.

"But mark this: There will be terrible times in the last days. People will be lovers of themselves, lovers of money, boastful, proud, abusive, disobedient to their parents, ungrateful, unholy, without love, unforgiving, slanderous, without self-control, brutal, not lovers of the good, treacherous, rash, conceited, lovers of pleasure rather than lovers of God—having a form of Godliness but denying its power. Have nothing to do with such people." 2 Timothy 3:1-5 (NIV)

- The world is changing fast—really fast!
- Believers shouldn't be surprised or unaware.

- We are here because God chose us to be, and he has allowed our current circumstance.
- Have faith in knowing He is aware.
- We must become people that God can use! (Don't hinder God.)
- Many people are confused about God.
- False Church. (Church people, but no power.)

So, instead of people seeking God they are watching us. (Watching *you!*) We are all that some see of God. Some people are learning about God from watching your life.

1. How you handle situations, challenges, problems, health issues and bad news?
2. Do they see gossip, and the practice of sin, complaining, lies, hopeless, rather than someone full of hope?

Blind Spots

"In the presence of God and of Christ Jesus, who will judge the living and the dead, and in view of his appearing and his kingdom, I give you this charge: Preach the word; be prepared in season and out of season; correct, rebuke and encourage—with great patience and careful instruction. For the time will come when people will not put up with sound doctrine. Instead, to suit their own desires, they will gather around them a great number of teachers to say what their itching ears want to hear. They will turn their ears away from the truth and turn aside to myths. But you, keep your head in all situations, endure hardship, do the work of an evangelist, discharge all the duties of your ministry."
2 Timothy 4:1-5 (NIV)

1. Choose Nice Buttercup Preaching—versus—Truth.
2. Block the Cross/Remove It from Sight—The Power.

Believers Must "Stand-Out" not "Blend-In."

I believe we will be held accountable for what God has called us to do here under the sun regardless of our circumstance, bad diagnosis, or tragic news. We are learning that Jesus loves us! We are important to Him.

- We are also learning that Jesus is King, Judge, Master! We must serve Him and play a role in His plans, not ours.
- Love God's people.
- Be calm; be stable; be happy; be considerate; be a *blessing.*
- Be joyful, not afraid of what is going on in the earth.
- Live the truth. Be positive!
- We may live on the earth, but our home is in the Kingdom of God.
- Focus on the Cross.
- Never let anyone remove Jesus or the Cross for your priorities.
- Understand that we serve a just God.
- There are consequences/rewards for our actions.
- Don't be an obstacle, be a vessel.

"You adulterous people, don't you know that friendship with the world means enmity against God? Therefore, anyone who chooses to be a friend of the world becomes an enemy of God." James 4:4 (NIV)

Second Peter 2:7-8 says, "And if He rescued Lot, a righteous man, who was distressed by the depraved conduct of the lawless (for that righteous man, living among them day after day, was tormented in His righteous soul by the lawless deeds he saw and heard). (NIV)

1. Believers should be uncomfortable "in the world."
2. Gossip, some music, dirty jokes, dirty movies, taking the Lord's name in vain, etc. should torment a believer and follower of Jesus.
3. Believers *must* stand out, not blend-in!
4. We must show great faith and courage in desperate and challenging times.

SET YOUR MIND:

- Set your mind on what you really want out of your life.
- Set your mind on who you are and whose you are.
- Satan can give you thoughts but he can't read your mind.
- Think good, positive thoughts and don't speak what you don't want.
- The enemy listens to you!

"Like a muddied spring or a polluted well are the righteous who give way to the wicked." Proverbs 25:26 (NIV)

1. Maintain your integrity, be authentic always.
2. Never give up!
3. Don't "water down" the truth.
4. Don't wink at untruths.
5. Eyes on the Cross, not on your diagnosis or tragic news.
6. Only one thing matters. The Cross!

"As Jesus was sitting on the Mount of Olives, the disciples came to him privately. 'Tell us,' They said, 'when will this happen, and what will be the sign of your coming and of the end of the age?'

"Jesus answered: 'Watch out that no one deceives you. For many will come in my name, claiming, 'I am the Messiah,' and will deceive many. You will hear of wars and rumors of wars, but see to it that you are not alarmed. Such things must happen, but the end is still to come. Nation will rise against nation, and kingdom against kingdom. There will be famines and earthquakes in various places. All these are the beginning of birth pains.

'Then you will be handed over to be persecuted and put to death, and you will be hated by all nations because of me. At that time many will turn away from the faith and will betray and hate each other, and many false prophets will appear and deceive many people. Because of the increase of wickedness, the love of most will grow cold, but the one who stands firm to the end will be saved. And this gospel of the kingdom will be preached in the whole world as a testimony to all nations, and then the end will come.'" Matthew 24:3-14 (NIV)

WHAT IS "NORMAL" TO YOU?

- Don't whine, blame, and complain.
- Don't waver.
- Remember you have the keys to bind and loose.
- Be the example regardless of your circumstance.
- Endure until the END!

CHAPTER 16

A FRESH START

"You're off to great places! Today is your day! Your mountain is waiting, So, get on your way!" —Dr. Seuss

Maybe you've quit a job, a relationship, or something by your own choosing, or perhaps you were let go or released not by your choice. Regardless, starting over always requires not only a leap of faith, but courage and endurance to face the future. After my retirement from the Air Force, I went through an identity shift. For twenty years my whole life was the Air Force and all at once that identity went away. I didn't know who I was. I had to start over and reinvent myself to Don Day 2.0.

Emotions can run high while energy and motivation can run low. Of course there's the excitement of new opportunities and the adventure ahead, but there's also insecurity and usually the fear of failure looming in your mind.

For a kickstart, we must first look back and deal with what happened. Too many times we have regrets or refuse to forgive ourselves for our past mistakes and choices. What's past is past, but we must deal with it first so we can move on. Maybe the change wasn't your idea.

The first step is to take inventory of what happened to end the situation and discern where things went wrong, why they failed and what part did you play in it. The objective here is to learn something from the experience so as not to make the same mistake again, to remove the regret that you may be feeling, to lift the blame, and to resolve the issue so it doesn't define you or your future. This inventory and review are to be brief and concise. Don't dwell on it over and over. The objective is to get a clear picture of the problem, solve it, and move on with your life.

"Sometimes you win…sometimes you learn." –John Maxwell

Maybe you are just in a rut and need motivation to get back in the game. Maybe because of a bad health diagnosis or tragic news, you and your life have changed forever. You need a fresh start. It happens to all of us some time or another. We need to set our minds on the good things ahead for us and not dwell on the bad. Staying positive is half the battle. New beginnings can be full of excitement, momentum, and enthusiasm if we see it that way. Our Kingdom view and perspective play a huge part in a fresh start.

The next step may sound strange, but hear me out: Be selfish for a season. To really start fresh, it may be past time to focus on yourself. So many of us are always helping everyone around us that we have a tendency to neglect ourselves at the expense of our physical or financial health. This is the time to give you the best chance at what's next and requires your best effort. You may need rest, therapy, some alone time, a change of scenery, or to be around some people that will encourage you and lift you up. This is an important time for you to prepare yourself to become all you can be on your new path. The world keeps spinning; there is no pause button. The new path is forward, not back.

Decide what type of fresh start you desire and need. What's it going to take to launch a fresh start? Knowing what you want in life makes it easier to take action. Knowing why you want the fresh start makes it sustainable. Remember for this short season the reboot of your life is all about you. Life has no pause button. No matter what happens life keeps spinning on. Life does have a reboot button; you just have to locate it and push reboot to restart your life.

There are two power tools in life and they are time and energy. It takes incredible effort to protect your time and make great trades with it. There is no such thing as saving time. When the clock strikes midnight it's the start of a new day and your daily allotment of 1,440 minutes begins. Once these precious minutes are spent, they never return. Trade wisely.

Our energy is the second power tool of life. To really get a fresh start it requires an enormous amount of energy to get you to where you want to be. Energy renews with results and momentum. The more successful you become the more energetic you become. Energy drains when you neglect to use your time wisely or when surrounded by energy-sucking people that want to see you back with them and away from your fresh start. Be alert and take action to remove yourself from them. After all, they are running on empty and you are fueled by the high octane of a fresh start.

It has taken me years to learn the art of a fresh start in my life. We all experience failures, challenges, loss, and rejections in our lives; it's normal. The more you live looking forward, the more opportunity you have to start over. You can't change the past, but you can change direction right now. If we allow the bad times to win, they seem to build on one another and pile up on us. But if we look at each week as a fresh start to try something new or go in a different direction soon the fresh starts outnumber the bad.

Make a bucket list of all the things you really want to do with your life. Maybe that is to travel to exotic places, learn a new language, finish your education, start your own business, make an impact on something bigger than you—like a charity, or run for political office. Live your life to the fullest. Don't settle. Why not *you*? It all starts with a thought, then an action step, and then you are that much closer to living your dreams. You can always find the time and a way if you focus your energy in that direction. You can do it. "You can. You will. You must!"

I love Mondays! They are a fresh start to a new week—a chance to forget what's behind and press onward toward the prize and what's next. I always tell my groups at my speaking events, "Remember to always try to get something from the day and not just try to get through the day. The world is happening for you not to you!" When you feel overwhelmed, just take a step back and start again. You have everything it takes to be uber-successful regardless of your current circumstance.

Where in your life have you had a failure or a setback? Why did it happen? What did you learn from it? Now set it free to live in the past where it belongs and make it a long distant faint memory and start fresh today. Walk through the steps and begin anew. You have a lot of life to live. Know this: The best of you is in the future not the past.

Chapter 17

GET OUT OF THE RUT!

"We all want success, but few want sacrifice."

Years ago, I read this story and it has stuck with me. I hope I can share it with you accurately. It will certainly resonate with the majority of those who read this book.

The story goes as follows: Charles Plumb was a US Navy jet pilot in Vietnam. After seventy-five combat missions, his plane was destroyed by a surface-to-air missile. Plumb ejected and parachuted into enemy hands. He was captured and spent six years in a communist Vietnamese prison. He survived the ordeal and now lectures on lessons learned from that experience.

One day, when Plumb and his wife were sitting in a restaurant, a man at another table came up and said, "You're Plumb! You flew jet fighters in Vietnam from the aircraft carrier Kitty Hawk. You were shot down!"

"How in the world did you know that?" asked Plumb.

"I packed your parachute," the man replied. Plumb gasped in surprise and gratitude. The man pumped his hand and said, "I guess it worked!"

Plumb assured him, "It sure did. If your chute hadn't worked, I wouldn't be here today."

Plumb couldn't sleep that night, thinking about that man. Plumb said, "I kept wondering what he might have looked like in a Navy uniform: a white hat, a bib in the back, and bell-bottom trousers. I wonder how many times I might have seen him and not even said, 'Good morning, how are you?' or anything because, you see, I was a fighter pilot and he was just a sailor."

Plumb thought of the manhours the sailor had spent on a long wooden table in the bowels of the ship, carefully weaving the shrouds and folding the silks of each chute, holding in his hands each time the fate of someone he didn't know.

Now, Plumb asks his audience, "Who's packing your parachute?" Everyone has someone who provides what they need to make it through the day. Plumb also points out that he needed many kinds of parachutes when his plane was shot down over enemy territory—he needed his physical parachute, his mental parachute, his emotional parachute, and his spiritual parachute. He called on all these supports before reaching safety.

Sometimes in the daily challenges that life gives us, we miss what is really important. We can get in a rut ourselves; in our own life and all we are dealing with. We can become blind to the world around us. We can easily become trapped in so many ways.

Look it's totally understandable, you get a bad diagnosis from your physician that you have a terminal illness. From that minute until who knows when, you can't hear or focus on anything but you and hopefully getting well. You become consumed with you.

We may fail to say hello, please, or thank you, or to congratulate someone on something wonderful that has happened to them, to give a compliment, or to just do something nice for no reason. We neglect to encourage others. Our focus is consumed with us.

No matter what your circumstance or challenge you are up against, do this as you go through this week, this month, this year—recognize people who pack your parachute. Thinking of others can help get you moving forward and upward. Pack someone's parachute this week.

Sometimes despite your best efforts to grow, mature, lose weight, or reach goals, you may experience stunted or sluggish growth. Here are some of the most common reasons for slow-to-no growth. For getting stuck in a rut!

FEAR OF LOSS IS GREATER THAN THE DESIRE FOR GAIN IN MOST OF US.

Here are some of the effects of fear:

- It can cause you to be in a rut!
- Fear can actually paralyze us.
- It causes us to make quick or bad decisions, or worse yet, no decision at all.
- Fear will cause us to settle for less or not take a calculated risk to exceed our goals.
- Fear makes us run from problems or confrontation, resulting in our being in a rut.
- Fear can cause us to be depressed or discouraged, and it zaps our energy!
- Fear will exhaust us, age us prematurely, steal our happiness, and cause us to be in a rut.

Some of you may be unhappy or unfulfilled in your life right now because there is something that you have been avoiding, not facing, hiding from, or not dealing with for a long time. News Flash: You will never be totally happy or fulfilled until you go back and deal with whatever has you in a rut. This requires repentance.

You may wonder, *What if I admit this and take responsibility? What will happen to me? What will people think or say about me?*

What people think about you is none of your business! We try to: Justify. Rationalize. Forget.

In how many areas in your life have you settled or been conditioned to accept less, and you're in a rut?

*Jealousy *Anger/Temper *Ungratefulness *Gossip *Unforgiveness *Unbelief *Greedy/Stingy *Complaining/ Whining *Lack of Integrity *Self-centered *Bad attitude

All of these will keep us "in a rut!"

Start with Telling the Truth. Stop Living a Lie. Stop Settling.

"But he said to me, 'My grace is sufficient for you, for my power is made perfect in weakness.' Therefore, I will boast all the more gladly about my weaknesses, so that Christ's power may rest on me. That is why, for Christ's sake, I delight in weaknesses, in insults, in hardships, in persecutions, in difficulties. For when I am weak, then I am strong." 2 Corinthians 12:9-10 (NIV)

Do away with all "time killers," that is, the stuff on your schedule that is robbing you of your time. People can and will suck the life and energy out of you by wasting your time. Cancel all unnecessary time wasters. Do it today.

Paul learned the secret of being an overcomer: Maintain God's perspective on the ups and downs of life, and access His power. The apostle was convinced that having the person of the Holy Spirit living *in* him meant that God's power was available *to* him.

BEWARE! The more you try to achieve, the more obstacles you'll face. The more you push the envelope, the harder it'll be to push through. The higher the stakes, the bigger the pitfalls you'll encounter. That's just how this sort of thing works.

You're not asking the right people the right questions—or you're not listening.

At the end of the day, this all comes down to one tremendously underrated quality, perseverance. If you're the kind of person who meets his/her commitments, who sticks with something through thick and thin, who never gives up and never surrenders, then I'm sure you'll become an overcomer.

Just showing up every day isn't enough. Do more—do something different!

Never forget who packed your parachute!

Chapter 18

Thanks to Derek Prince for his knowledge and teaching on this topic. He has greatly influenced my understanding.

YOU CAN BE DELIVERED FROM EVIL SPIRITS AND THEIR DEMONIC INFLUENCE

"For we do not wrestle against flesh and blood, but against principalities, against powers, against the rulers of darkness in this age, against spiritual hosts of wickedness in high places."
Ephesians 6:12 (NKJV)

The Bible says we do not battle against flesh and blood, but it seems to me all of my problems come with skin on them. Anyone not aware can have demonic influence in their life.

You See the Spirit of the Anti-Christ Is Already in the Earth.

When you receive a bad diagnosis or tragic news, rest assured Satan will send his angels to begin to destroy you. He will ambush you with fear, doubt, worry, and many other evil attacks. He wants to knock you off your path. Evil never sleeps.

"Just then a man in their synagogue who was possessed by an impure spirit cried out, 'What do you want with us, Jesus of Nazareth? Have you come to destroy us? I know who you are—the Holy One of God!'

"'Be quiet!' said Jesus sternly. 'Come out of him!' The impure spirit shook the man violently and came out of him with a shriek.

"The people were all so amazed that they asked each other, 'What is this? A new teaching—and with authority! He even gives orders to impure spirits and they obey him.' News about him spread quickly over the whole region of Galilee." Mark 1:23-28 (NIV)

One of the Earliest Recorded Miracles in Jesus' Earthly Ministry

The demon described in Mark 1 knew exactly who Jesus was. Jesus spoke directly to the demonic spirit and commanded him to come out of the man. This was Spirit-to-spirit contact between Jesus and the demon. The unclean evil spirit came out of the man. They were all amazed.

Jesus Was Known as the Man Who Could Cast Out Evil Spirits.

"That evening after sunset the people brought to Jesus all the sick and demon-possessed. The whole town gathered at the door, and Jesus healed many who had various diseases. He also drove out many demons, but He would not let the demons speak because they knew who He was." Mark 1:32-34 (NIV)

The same evening—they were demonized, not demon possessed. *Possessed* means ownership. If you are a believer, you can't be owned by Satan, but you can be demonized. You can see it all around you.

The people came from all over to be healed of their sickness and in providing healing for them, Jesus cast out many demons. Many demons are the cause for many sicknesses, and in many cases, to be delivered from a sickness you must first be delivered from the demon.

I believe God can and will heal me of Parkinson's. He can use doctors, medicine, treatment, or speak it gone. I'm fine with any and all of them.

> "So he traveled throughout Galilee, preaching in their synagogues and driving out demons." Mark 1:39 (NIV)

JESUS CAST OUT MANY DEMONS EVERYWHERE HE PREACHED.

"Moreover, demons came out of many people, shouting, 'You are the Son of God!' But he rebuked them and would not allow them to speak, because they knew He was the Messiah."
Luke 4:41 (NIV)

As evidenced in the Bible, Jesus never separated preaching and casting out demons. Demons are the causes of many sicknesses and problems. Some directly or some indirectly through attitudes that prevents them from receiving healing through faith or unbelief.

We have gotten away from this so a lot of people who need deliverance don't get it and a lot of people that need healing don't get it. In many cases casting out demons and pulling down strongholds must be done first before anything else can happen. When I'm asked to pray for someone physically,

I always asked where is this person spiritually. Physical health is not worth much if you are spiritually unhealthy or dead. I always want to get them spiritually fit first.

"On a Sabbath Jesus was teaching in one of the synagogues, and a woman was there who had been crippled by a spirit for eighteen years. She was bent over and could not straighten up at all. When Jesus saw her, he called her forward and said to her, 'Woman, you are set free from your infirmity.' Then he put his hands on her, and immediately she straightened up and praised God." Luke 13:11-13 (NIV)

It looks like a physical problem, but it was caused by an evil spirit of infirmity. Jesus didn't pray for healing, He dealt with the spirit of infirmity. The real cause was demonic.

"Then should not this woman, a daughter of Abraham, whom Satan has kept bound for eighteen long years, be set free on the Sabbath day from what bound her?" Luke 13:16 (NIV)

"He replied, 'Go tell that fox, 'I will keep on driving out demons and healing people today and tomorrow, and on the third day I will reach my goal.'" Luke 13:32 (NIV)

"Jesus called His twelve disciples to him and gave them authority to drive out impure spirits and to heal every disease and sickness." Matthew 10:1(NIV)

"These twelve Jesus sent out with the following instructions: 'Do not go among the Gentiles or enter any town of the Samaritans. Go rather to the lost sheep of Israel. As you go, proclaim this message: 'The kingdom of heaven has come near.' Heal the sick, raise the dead, cleanse those who have leprosy, drive out demons. Freely you have received; freely give.'" Mathew 10:5-8 (NIV)

Jesus prepared and equipped everyone He sent out to evangelize and deal with demonic influence in his name. They had authority over the demons in Jesus's powerful name.

"Lord even the demons are subject to us in Your name! Amen."

"Then Jesus came to them and said, 'All authority in heaven and on earth has been given to me. Therefore go and make disciples of all nations, baptizing them in the name of the Father and of the Son and of the Holy Spirit, and teaching them to obey everything I have commanded you. And surely, I am with you always, to the very end of the age.'" Matt. 28:18-20 (NIV)

Teach other disciples to cast out demons, somewhere we stopped teaching.

"The seventy-two returned with joy and said, 'Lord, even the demons submit to us in your name.'" Luke 10:17 (NIV)

Evil spirits are persons. We have to discern if we are dealing with a demon or our earthly flesh. So many times, we give blame or credit to evil spirits when it's our selfish flesh that's to blame.

"And everyone who calls on the name of the Lord will be saved; for on Mount Zion and in Jerusalem there will be deliverance, as the Lord has said, even among the survivors whom the Lord calls." Joel 2:32 (NIV)

Three Objectives of Demons

1. Torment and torture.
2. To keep you from knowing Christ as Savior.
3. To keep you from serving Christ.

We must distinguish between evil spirit and flesh. Satan gets way too much credit for our selfish ambition, poor choices, and practice of sin. We must stop it.

Demons:

1. Entice
2. Harass
3. Torment (physically and mentally)
4. Compel/tempt us to do things we really don't want to do
5. Enslave (placing us in bondage like addictions)
6. Defile (encouraging lust and unclean thoughts)
7. Deceive (through false prophets, false church, and false miracles)
8. Make people sick, tired, depressed, and sleepless
9. Knock us off our path

Prayer: Heavenly Father, we ask you to forgive us where we have sinned and fallen short of what you demand. We humble ourselves and acknowledge you as: King of Kings, Lord of Lords, Creator of All Things, the One True Living God, the Beginning and the End. Only by Your grace and through Your truth we have found freedom and deliverance. Let the darkness be pushed back and the light breakthrough in this season. Help us to be self-controlled and alert as the enemy the devil prowls around looking for someone to devour. Satan targets us through our family, finance, and our health. Thank You for the authority to rebuke him and cast out every evil spirit that wants to cause us harm, even death. In Jesus's name, amen.

Chapter 19

PRESSING TOWARD THE GOAL

"Burn Your Boats!"

We've all heard the story about Spanish conquistador Hernán Cortés who issued a bizarre order to his 600 men as they began their conquest of the Aztec empire in 1519. The order was abrupt and concise: "Burn the Boats."

Legend has it that they were outnumbered by the Aztecs 100-1. Also, that many had tried to conquer the Aztec empire and all have failed. So, something new must be attempted; something drastic to increase the odds that while outnumbered they could still win.

Where in your life do you feel outnumbered? Where do you feel the odds are stacked against you. Do you feel you need a Plan B, C, D, and E?

"Burn the Boats!" He wanted his men to know that they had no opportunity to retreat, so they had fight with everything they had, losing was not an option. With failure no longer an option; winning this battle became the most important thing to them. It was their only focus. Win or die, no other options.

Just think about your current life conditions. Have you come to the conclusion that losing is not an option. This is where you need a do-or-die, a burn-the-boats, or a no-turning-back-attitude.

Over the years I've read or heard many stories about, "burn the boats." Some say it never happened, some say they sunk the boats not burned them, and many other variations of the tale. Regardless of the story what I took away from it was this: "Retreat or quitting is easy when it's an option." Think about that for a moment. We all hang onto something as our parachute, escape route, Plan B our exit plan just in case things get more difficult than we would like.

So many of us operate our life based and directed on fear or pain. So, we postpone any action until we no longer feel fear or pain which may or may not happen. Living your life by fear and feelings is a miserable way to live.

"Not that I have already attained, or am already perfected; but I press on, that I may lay hold of that for which Christ Jesus has also laid hold of me. Brethren, I do not count myself to have apprehended; but one thing I do, forgetting those things which are behind and reaching forward to those things which are ahead, I press toward the goal for the prize of the upward call of God in Christ Jesus." Philippians 3:12-14

During the last five years I have spoken to thousands of attendees at my events. Hundreds of them have told me, "I wish, I can't, I never, I would love to—" I say, "Oh, really, tell me about all of the attempts and things you have tried and failed at that thing. How long have you been trying?" Their answer is usually, none! They haven't even tried or stepped out in faith one time. They prefer to just talk and not act on it. They are "daytime talkers."

I always like to give at least two applications at all of my events, and I'll give them to you, too.

TWO THINGS THAT YOU CAN IMPLEMENT RIGHT NOW TODAY TO IMPROVE YOUR CURRENT AND FUTURE LIFE CONDITIONS ARE:

1. **Stop doing stupid stuff.** If you ever start an activity with, "Hey Watch this..." it's a sign that something stupid is about to happen. Stop and think it through. We do stupid stuff even though we know better. Stop it!
2. **Do what you already know to do:** Eat healthy, get some exercise, save some money, invest in yourself, keep growing, be generous, and build stronger relationships. We know what we should do so much that we end up *should*-ing all over ourselves.

The secret I share is that you aren't "going" through something, but you are *growing* through it. They just need to go "all in!" You just need to, "burn the boats!"

Are you ready to burn some boats? What boats do you need to burn in your life right now? Where are you hanging on to that which is diminishing to you and your life conditions? What safety net or training wheels do you need to remove right now? You know your Plan B that you can always use as an escape when things get difficult. This always leads to settling or quitting.

At some point, for you to grow and succeed in any area of your life, you need to commit to a mindset that failure is not an option—that you have no boat to retreat to. If you are always planning with a backup plan in mind, you have already failed at some level.

When retreat is not an option, you will get up every morning and make decisions, focus on the steps and take action for your life today one step at a time. After all, you are all in and no other options but to win. This plan requires courage and action regardless of your current situation.

Burning the boats represents a point of no return, a commitment to going through a door you can never turn back from. There is no negotiation, no looking back, but now all of your focus, thoughts, momentum, and efforts will be pointed to succeeding in this one commitment in your life.

So often, I see many wannabes real estate agents holding on to their other jobs while trying to set up new real estate practice. To me this represents a lack of faith in their own abilities, commitment and their faith that they can succeed in the real estate industry. They have one foot on the land and the other foot on the burning boat. This is the formula for a bad day.

They think this plan of holding on to a life line or safety net will save them if they can't do it, but they are actually diminishing their opportunity to succeed. They also diminish their value in their current position because their focus is divided. When you chase two rabbits usually, they both get away.

I believe in never burning bridges, but I also understand and agree with burning your boats. It means to go all in and focus all of your plan, talent, effort, resources, on your target and have a no turning back policy.

We have been programmed over the years by "this is how we do it" or "this is the way we've always done it." Go to school, get a job, get married, get a mortgage, and save money for retirement. Then retire, and if you have saved enough money and are healthy you can then travel some or enjoy your golden years. If this is total success for you then you have already burned your boats in a sense. If this is not your idea of success you need to burn your boats and win at your dreams and passion. You are an overcomer. Never give up on life. God has ordained your days. Ignore the naysayers and your current circumstance and start playing BIG!

All change happens first with a thought, then a decision, and finally a commitment to change. You may want change your body, eliminate debt, start a new career, or finish your education, training or certification. The most critical step to change is that after the decision to change it's the action you take to make the change happen. Change has to take place on the inside first.

I've heard speakers and coaches say, "Fake it till you make it!" Sorry, I don't believe you should fake anything, let alone your life. Don't go into debt to look the part or to live a lie. Be the best you, you can be. Work hard, learn much and act on your new found knowledge. You are the best *you* anyone could ever be. Believe in *you!* I do.

When you make a commitment decision, one you can't go back on because you are completely sold out, all in, totally surrendered to making it do what you decided for it to do. Few of us reach this level of commitment, but for those special few they not only change their life and the lives of their family and community, they just might change our life too. All because they decided to burn the boats!

If You Really Want It, Burn YOUR Boats and Get Going

Where in your life do you need a fresh start? What dream, or purpose are you willing to fully commit to. What boats must you burn to insure you will not turn back? When will you take the first step toward your dreams and start living your dream and not someone else's?

1. **Identify your boats!** Your boat is your excuse for not going all in. What is your safety net? What is your Plan B? When you have something that is a *must-do,* you will have to burn your boat to improve your chances of success. No turning back and no quitting.

> It is easy to say that you want to change, but the real challenge is to actually do it. Once again, there is a choice. You can plan, talk about your goals with people, wish that everything will work out the way you want it to—or you can start acting right now. Choose to be assertive and bold regardless of your current circumstance.

Go after your goals with grit and determination. Don't let the naysayers hold you back from your dreams. Read self-help books and listen to thoughtful podcasts to pump you up and learn new skills and the means to becoming a better more successful person. If you want a new job, put together a résumé, contact recruiters, respond to job listings, network and do everything in your power to make it happen. If you like your company, but feel overlooked, schedule a meeting with your boss and tell her of your ambitions, all the qualities you have to offer and ask how you can advance within the organization because you can do all things through him who gives you strength.

2. **What makes it so difficult to burn: fear?** Comfort? Lack of confidence in yourself? Identify the barrier so you can remove it, go around it, go over it, or go through it.

3. **Have you ever burned a boat in the past?** How did that workout? What did you learn?

Think about how you spend your day, the people you regularly associate with and the way you view things. Do your friends, co-workers and family drag you down? Are they negative and unsupportive of your dreams? Who ya' hangin with; chickens or eagles?

What do you do with your free time? Do you read books, stay up on developments within your industry and try to grow intellectually—or do you waste your precious time on shopping on Amazon, playing video games, or watching TV?

Do you have a positive mindset or do you view life in a negative and critical attitude? If you truly want to become more successful, you will need to address these and related questions honestly. If you feel that certain friends or relatives are hampering your development, you may need to have a serious conversation with them or start seeing less of them. Substitute these types of people with those who are positive, motivated, uplifting and pray for you to succeed. Start working on becoming smarter and more knowledgeable about your work.

4. **Transform your "should do" into "must-do."** *Burning your boats* represents a point of no return, a commitment to crossing a line you can never turn back from. "Must" is used to mark a necessity or non-negotiable. It is used when people are determined to do something. "You can. You will. You must!"

   "Must" represents more of a covenant while "should" represents a possibility. We usually end up *should-ing* all over ourselves.

   There is no more second guessing. From now on all thoughts and actions must be focused on succeeding in your new reality. Ditch the backup camera and rear-view mirror. No more reverse only forward.

5. **Safety nets and escape routes** can protect us from pain and injury, but they also will reduce the effort, focus, and the commitment we expend in the process. Once you have made a choice, you have to be willing to burn the boats behind you…it's a MUST-do!

6. **Trust your inner voice.** Pursue your dreams. Never retreat.

> "Our deepest fear is not that we are inadequate. Our deepest fear is that we are powerful beyond measure. It is our light, not our darkness that most frightens us. We ask ourselves, *Who am I to be brilliant, gorgeous, talented, fabulous?* Actually, who are you *not* to be? You are a child of God. Playing small does not serve the world. There is nothing enlightened about shrinking so that other people won't feel insecure around you. We are all meant to shine, as children do. We were born to make manifest the glory of God that is within us. It's not just in some of us; it's in everyone. And as we let our own light shine, we unconsciously give other people permission to do the same. As we are liberated from our own fear, our presence automatically liberates others." —Marianne Williamson

You Are Capable of So Much More in Life … Don't Settle … BURN THE BOATS!

Chapter 20

INVINCIBILITY!

"Take My yoke upon you and learn from me ..."
Matthew 11:29 (NIV)

Becoming I-N-V-I-N-C-B-I-L-E and knowing the difference between God's plan and ours.

Many of us are expert complainers. Our Lord begins to bring us to the point where we can have fellowship with Him, only to hear us moan and groan, saying, "Oh, Lord, just let me be like other people! Let me have this or that. I never get anything I want or pray for."

Jesus is asking us to get beside Him and take one end of the yoke, so that we can pull together. That's why Jesus says to us, "My yoke is easy and my burden is light." Matthew 11:30

God takes us off of our emotional roller coaster, and then our complaining turns into praise and worship. The only way to know the strength of God is to take the yoke of Jesus and to learn from Him. We learn by doing: LBD. We learn by trusting.

We must remember we serve at His pleasure not ours. We work out His plan and purpose, not ours. Just because you got a bad diagnosis or bad news or in a diminished position, or in a less than desired circumstance doesn't mean you get to cry, moan and complain forever. You must learn to be more concerned about God's plan than your relief. "... the joy of the LORD is your strength." Nehemiah 8:10 (NIV)

No power on earth or in hell can conquer the Spirit of God living within the human spirit; it creates an inner invincibility. It is definitely a crime and disgrace for a Christian to be weak in God's strength. It's more about your spiritual health than your physical health or circumstance. To endure and persevere till the end, you will need your spiritual health and the power of the Holy Spirit.

Accept His Power and the Authority He Has Given to You

Overall, I think that you have to give God all of you, because anything less than all is as good as nothing of you. In order to give all of yourself to God, which means everything that you give Him must be based internally, which branches to the external. If you only give Him the external, then it's like giving him just the part of the fruit instead of the whole fruit itself.

This includes your mind, especially your mind. The mind is where the battlefield is. He requires us to give our mind over to him through thought, understanding, and action.

It's confusing, but I feel all you need to do when things get complicated as you get to the bottom line is to just focus on building a closer relationship with Christ and then surrender to His plan. You aren't ways right, but He is! You can trust Him!

God's Will or Your Will?

Even if you don't understand God's plan, you need to respond to His instruction. In fact, when you don't understand God's plan, it is even more important to do exactly what He directs us to do. God wants you to decide in advance, to just trust Him and believe that His plan is the best plan for your life.

Most of the time, God asks us to make the choice to do His will before we know the specific details of His plan. (Ever happen to you?) That's because part of God's plan is to develop in us a trust of His character and His grace. (How well do you know the Father?)

You must know the original so you don't get deceived by the counterfeit. I recently went to the grocery store and gave the cashier two $100 bills for my groceries. She took a marker and drew a line on each bill and then she held each bill up in the light to verify that the bills were real and not counterfeit. Wouldn't it be great to have a marker to use on people we come in contact with to determine if they are real or not?

Many of us get into a battle of wills with God, wanting Him to reveal His plan to us first and only then will we decide whether or not to do what He tells us to do.

We ask all of our friends what they think is happening and what should you do. This is a case of the blind leading the blind. You'll both fall into a ditch.

But that's not the way it works. God wants you to decide in advance, trusting Him and believing that His Will is the best plan for your life, believing that He will strengthen you to do all that He asks you to do.

One reason God doesn't give you the full picture of His plans for your life is that you may be overwhelmed by what you see. (You can't handle the truth). For instance, it may appear impossible for you to complete everything he plans for you during this season. But that's the point—there's no way you can fulfill your mission without God empowering you. (We need God to do God stuff.)

Prayer: Heavenly Father, you bestow honor and authority according to Your great wisdom and understanding. Help me to order my days so that Your very best will fill my future. I turn my heart to You to learn and trust Your ways, character, and plan. Help me serve and seek You each day. Grant me a willing spirit. Let the name of Jesus be held in high honor throughout the earth, amen.

CHAPTER 21

A DAY OF WAR

"When you're interested in something you'll do whatever is convenient. When you are committed, you'll do whatever it takes."

"Your troops will be willing on your day of battle. Arrayed in holy majesty, from the womb of the dawn your young men will come to you like the dew." Psalm 110:3 (NIV)

Remember that God is a God of war. Scripture makes it clear that the present age is going to close with a tremendous battle between the forces of God and the forces of Satan and God is gathering His army. It says, "Your troops will be willing in your day of battle."

God doesn't want us to give Him something. He wants us to give Him ourselves—not our talents, not our time, not our strength—just ourselves. We are to be the free-will offerings. And it says, "From the womb of the dawn your young men will come to you like the dew." God is gathering an army of young people today.

The end times are upon us. It started with the New Testament and has continued on since then. While it hasn't happened already, soon our very existence will be threatened and we will have to make a choice in how we will respond. First, we can respond in fear by choosing to stay in our comfortable space and believe that it will never truly impact us personally. We can also hide out in fear, just waiting for Jesus's return. I believe we need to prepare for the worst and pray for the best.

Next, we can deny that the signs of the end times are happening all around us. There's also the option of becoming focused on self-protection so that we are not focused on others or we can do the opposite by becoming passive, believing the lie that things are so bad, there's nothing we can do to make an impact. This is called deception. When we are in a diminished position it's easy to hide from reality because all of our focus is on us and our circumstance. We are easily deceived.

Then, there's the final option. We can start using the spiritual weapons of warfare that God has given us. As believers, we are engaged in spiritual battle. The enemy wants to stop the fulfillment of God's promises and knock you off your path. In these uncertain end times, it's important that we are equipped with practical strategies to defeat the enemy. We have the power of the Holy Spirit to empower us to endure untill the end.

Here are five spiritual weapons for the end times, based on the book *Spiritual Warfare for the End Times* by Derek Prince.

God's Word

God's Word is the most powerful spiritual weapon for the end times. It's important that we use His Word to combat the enemy and all his evil forces. Prince points out that in order to overcome evil, we must be alive in Christ—having access to God's resources, wisdom, power, and the weapons he has placed at our disposal.

"In order to overcome evil, we must be acquainted with the Bible," Prince says. "We must know what the Bible teaches about evil. We must also know the provision God has made for us to overcome evil."

Most people don't know how to use the Word of God against the devil—even people who have been in the church for years who have heard the Word the whole time. But hearing the Word isn't the same as using the Word. Being able to use God's Word against Satan is one of the most important marks of spiritual maturity. Begin with key verses in areas where you're often tempted. Then, when you're tempted, you'll be able to use God's Word against Satan and win.

TESTIFYING

Revelation 12:11 points out the spiritual weapons we must utilize: "And they [believers on earth] overcome him [Satan] by the blood of the Lamb and by the word of their testimony, and they did not love their lives to the death."

This is the same Lamb pointed out in John 1:29 who takes away the sin of the world. Prince says, "Testifying is the personal action that makes this truth operative. If we do not testify, nothing goes into operation. Our personal testimony is the action that triggers the whole process and brings Satan's defeat."

When we begin to testify the Word of God, we experience a special kind of opposition and begin to do the devil harm. The devil is fine with us believing whatever we like to believe until we begin to share our testimony. That's when he really gets rattled. When you do this, the enemy will do everything he can to frighten and discourage you because He wants to keep you from declaring the Word of God. Satan wants to knock you off your path. But your testimony has greater power!

PRAYER

Prayer is an incredibly powerful spiritual weapon. It's hardly a coincidence that the weapons of God's Word and prayer are listed concurrently in Ephesians 6. While the Word itself is powerful and prayer is absolutely essential, combining the two is even more powerful still.

As we abide in Him and His Word abides in us, we can more confidently pray His Will, enabling us to battle the enemy. This doesn't mean we need spend hours in prayer each day it is simply a time to remind yourself who you are and where you get your strength.

"You remind yourself of what Christ has done to the devil and the fact that the devil has no right of access to you," Prince says. "You and I can serve Jesus without fear, having been delivered from the hands of our enemies." The only power Satan has over you is what you give him. He is already defeated.

Too often, people are praying ineffective prayers that can't be answered because they are asking for what God has already given them. We are in a war and we need to pray like it.

GIFTS OF THE HOLY SPIRIT

In order to defeat the kingdom of darkness, God equips us with supernatural tools. One of those tools is the Holy Spirit. Prince writes, "God's intention is to restore to His people the gifts of the Holy Spirit. They are the tools and weapons that are needed for doing the work."

When a Christian is equipped with the power of the Holy Spirit, they have more power and more spiritual authority in them than all the power of the enemy. We have been given divinely powerful weapons. Use them. It's more difficult when we are absorbed and focused with our individual problems or circumstances. We must give our undivided attention to God and his plan, not our relief or circumstance.

Few understand how to use them. It's so important that this changes. Those who do not understand and walk in this authority, and know how to use these divinely powerful weapons, will find themselves in increasingly difficult situations and even jeopardy. The Lord gave us the armor and the weapons of our warfare because we need them.

FORGIVENESS

One major and common reason why believers give Satan a legal claim in their lives is their failure to forgive others, Prince says. Jesus taught us that we are forgiven by God to the same degree we forgive others. "Forgive us our debts, as we forgive our debtors." Matthew 6:12 (NIV)

The truth is, we can't claim forgiveness from God beyond the measure to which we forgive others. Prince explains, "Essentially, when we refuse to forgive others, we allow Satan to have yet another legal claim. Do what you will, you cannot dislodge him until you have forgiven the one you need to forgive."

The devil is a legal expert and he knows it. The good news is God's Word offers total forgiveness of sin and it is more imperative now than ever that we hold on to the total forgiveness by faith.

The apostle Paul taught, "The weapons of our warfare are not carnal, but mighty through God to the pulling down of strongholds." (2 Corinthians 10:4) This promise is life-changing, meaning the difference for us between victory and defeat during the coming days. As the world gets darker and darker around us and we face greater spiritual battles than ever before, we have hope through Jesus Christ. Put on the full armor of God, trust in His Word and use these spiritual weapons that will prepare you for the end times.

Prayer: Heavenly Father, we humble ourselves before You tonight to acknowledge You as Creator of all things. Because of You who strengthens us we can do all things. You made us and chose us; we are the sheep of Your pasture. Help us to be obedient to You as Your warriors. Help us to be self-controlled and alert. The enemy the devil prowls around like a roaring lion looking for someone to devour. Help us resist him and stand form in the faith, in Jesus's name, amen.

Chapter 22

THE FAMILY'S PERSPECTIVE AND STRUGGLE: SHELLY DAY, WIFE AND OVERCOMER

I'm a happily married woman of forty-six years to my high school sweetheart. I usually have a very positive outlook on life and about any situation. Nothing could have prepared me for the news, "Your husband has Parkinson's disease." I always thought we would live out our days together being active and healthy like we have always been.

What was your immediate response your health diagnosis or bad news?

Total disbelief and fear of the future. Afraid for what this evil disease could do to my husband. Don has always been an optimist, glass overflowing, endurance athlete, and a motivate others type of guy. Now we were facing uncharted waters.

WHAT ACTIONS DID YOU TAKE THE NEXT SEVERAL DAYS?

I consider myself a prayer warrior who trusts in the Lord Jesus Christ. I invite the Holy Spirit into every detail of my life each day, to lead and direct my path. So, I put a plan into motion the very day of Don's diagnosis to not dwell on what I might see, but rather to pray and believe that the Lord would lift this diagnosis off of my husband. That has been my prayer and continues to be every day. We walk this out one day at a time.

WHAT THOUGHTS FLOODED YOUR MIND DURING THE FIRST FEW WEEKS?

I remember early one morning sitting in our sunroom which has windows facing every direction. So many thoughts were running through my mind as I was looking toward the east, about the break of dawn and I saw what looked like the bottom of a huge hand. I went outside to see it more clearly. As I looked up, I knew in my Spirit that it was a sign from the Lord. It was the largest hand I have ever seen and for the first time in weeks I had immediate peace. I knew the scriptures in Psalms 46:1 and 91, "God is a refuge and strength an ever-present help in times of trouble" which gives us peace and "he that dwells in the secret place of the most High shall abide under the shadow of the Almighty."

WHAT ADVICE WOULD YOU GIVE SOMEONE IN A SIMILAR SITUATION TO BECOME AN OVERCOMER?

Take each morning and say to the Lord: "I give it to you and won't take it back." Let Him fight the battle under His strength not yours. Don't look beyond today and cherish every hour you have together with your loved one.

Psalm 55:22 says, "Cast your cares on the LORD and he will sustain you; He will never let the righteous be shaken" (NIV). Believe the promises of God. He loves you.

WHAT IS YOUR LONG-TERM PLAN FOR YOUR LIFE?

To continue to lean-in and trust the Lord for our future. The Lord knows our circumstances now and into the future and we can trust him. I will invest my days ahead being grateful and thankful for what the Lord has done and will do for Don and me. We will continue to praise the Lord and enjoy every day we have together. We are overcomers.

CHRIS DAY, SON AND OVERCOMER

My name is Chris Day. I am Don's son and business partner. I am a positive, consistent, disciplined, and encouraging person. I am married to my best friend, Emily, and we have a sweet son, Finley, and a loving border collie, Rhoda. My profession allows me to engage with people in the joy of home ownership through buying and selling real estate. I enjoy spending time with family, friends, and my Orangetheory Fitness 5AM crew.

WHAT WAS YOUR IMMEDIATE RESPONSE TO YOUR DAD'S HEALTH DIAGNOSIS OR BAD NEWS?

My immediate response to receiving the news of my father having Parkinson's disease was at first shock. I felt like maybe he was just having symptoms from stress or being tired, but surely not Parkinson's. However, my father is an overcomer and loves the Lord, so he knows that he doesn't have to fight this disease alone. My father has always taught to endure and never give up.

I remember throughout my childhood my dad ran a lot of races sometimes every weekend. I can remember hundreds of races but I can't recall a single race where he quit. We never give up! We can always ask why things happen, but it doesn't take away the fact that difficult things will happen in life and your mindset is so important to overcoming the difficult things as they happen.

WHAT ACTIONS DID YOU TAKE THE NEXT SEVERAL DAYS?

At the time, I personally didn't know anyone with this disease near me and so I would need to take time and learn and listen. I am firm believer in the Lord and prayer so, I lifted my dad up in prayer and knew that God will walk with him, just like our family throughout each day of his life. I wanted to show him support and make him aware that although his body and ability to do some things as he once did may change, his mind is still very sharp and he can do hard things.

For most of his life my dad has been an endurance athlete with a strong mind and body. I believe this will serve him well in the coming years. He knows how to endure.

WHAT THOUGHTS FLOODED YOUR MIND DURING THE FIRST FEW WEEKS?

The first few weeks I thought that I wanted to be available to my father by encouraging him and assisting him where he needed help. My father and I work together so this was easier for me than most. We've always had a great relationship and this disease wasn't going to bring us down, but instead closer and stronger together. We fight this disease one day at a time.

WHAT ADVICE/INFORMATION WOULD YOU GIVE SOMEONE WITH A SIMILAR SITUATION TO BE AN OVERCOMER?

Life is hard and it's a long run, not a sprint, and in order to really have joy and strength it must come from somewhere other than yourself. I've learned and give full credit my strength and joy come from the Lord. He will guide you and direct your paths if you'll let him.

Knowledge is power when you take action on it. Learn all you can about things from a reliable and positive source. Keep your head up and feet down. Never, ever quit.

WHAT IS YOUR LONG-TERM PLAN FOR YOUR LIFE?

My long-term plan for my life is to enjoy each day I have because tomorrow isn't promised. Tell others how important they are to me and to be where your feet are! Our time is the most valuable resource we have, and it is so important to be intentional about the time we spend doing things. I am going to make sure to stay on top of my health through my fitness and be aware of any warning signs, because life can change in just a matter of minutes.

SHANNON BARRETT, DAUGHTER AND OVERCOMER

My name is Shannon and I am Don's daughter. I'm married with three children, a dog, and a cat, so there are always somethings to do every day. My dad has always been a constant in my life. He is someone I could always trust and turn to with any challenge, question, or need. He was always there for me and the rest of our family. I feel very blessed he is my dad and Papa to my children.

WHAT WAS YOUR IMMEDIATE RESPONSE TO HIS HEALTH DIAGNOSIS OR BAD NEWS?

When my dad told me about his diagnosis of Parkinson's disease my first reaction was sadness, which shifted to being on an emotional roller coaster. I had so many emotions and confusion of why has this happened to my dad and our family. I felt angry. My dad took the news well and seemed confident that he would fight this disease and win. He has always been positive and encouraging.

WHAT ACTIONS DID YOU TAKE THE NEXT SEVERAL DAYS?

I prayed a lot and asked myself why was this happening? How did he get this cruel disease? Being able to talk with our family helped. I also did a lot of research about the disease. I found a lot of information, but no cure. Deep in my heart I just wanted to help my dad in any way I could. I come to the conclusion that "why" didn't matter as much as "what now and what next" does.

WHAT THOUGHTS FLOODED YOUR MIND DURING THE FIRST FEW WEEKS?

I was numb and it was difficult to think clearly. I felt helpless but not hopeless. I wasn't sure of what to say or do to help my dad. I only knew I wanted my dad to be healthy and live a quality life. My thoughts turned to my mom. What must she be going through and what is she feeling and how is she dealing with this disease. I watched her walking beside my dad as they faced this disease together. They have always been a close team and now it was more important than ever.

WHAT ADVICE/INFORMATION WOULD YOU GIVE SOMEONE WITH A SIMILAR SITUATION TO BE AN OVERCOMER?

I would first tell them to go to God with it all and tell him everything they are going through. Ask God for help, guidance, wisdom, discernment and just be honest withhHim. He knows your heart any way. God is your only answer. I am thankful I have a great family; we love and support each other through the good times and not so good times. We serve a God who can order our steps one step at a time.

WHAT IS YOUR LONG-TERM PLAN FOR YOUR LIFE?

My plan is to live out every day to the fullest that God has ordained for me. I want to spend as much time with my dad as possible and help him live his best life every day doing all the things he loves. I want my children to hang out with their Papa and GiGi as often as possible. I am very proud of my dad's endurance, faith, and perseverance as he battles this evil Parkinson's disease. He is a true overcomer. I love you, Dad!

CHAPTER 23

LIVING CERTAIN IN AN UNCERTAIN WORLD!

Life is but a vapor. We are here today and gone tomorrow. We know not our date or time of passing. Death is only a reminder.

I heard of a great statistic: Ten out of ten people die! So, what are we going to do? What should we do? What is the *best* practice to get the most out of this brief life and operate at our true potential?

A life of uncertainty creates pressure and stress. Our objective should be to achieve unshakeable power and peace of mind in a world of uncertainty.

> **un·shake·able:** An unwavering and undisputed confidence; a steadfast commitment to the truth; presence, peace of mind, and a calm in the middle of the storm. (Calm, collected, composed, coolheaded, icy, nonchalant, self-collected, self-composed, self-possessed, serene, steely, tranquil, undisturbed, unruffled, unshaken, untroubled, unworried).

What would it feel like to know in your mind, in your heart, and in the very depth of your soul that you'll always be successful? To know with absolute certainty that no matter what happens in the economy, stock market, or real estate, you'll have security and peace of mind for the rest of your life?

Look, I know if you are reading this book, you have personally suffered an attack of some kind that has you spinning in all directions. You feel vulnerable and possibly defeated. Me too! But you can overcome your current challenge. This, too, has come to pass, not come to stay. It will require you to surrender it all to God and seek out His plan and purpose, not your suffering. Then you will begin to see the unshakeable path.

To know that you'll possess abundance that will enable you not only to take care of your family's needs but also to delight in the joy of helping others.

We all desire and dream of being unshakeable. But what does it really mean to be unshakeable? It's not just a matter of money or being financially secure. It's a state of mind. When you're truly unshakeable, you have unwavering confidence even in the middle of the storm.

It's not that nothing upsets you. We all go through challenges under the sun. We are either *in* a challenge, coming *out* of a challenge, or going *into* a *new* challenge.

But you don't stay there. Nothing rattles you for any length of time. You don't allow fear to take you over. If you're knocked off balance, you find your center quickly and regain your inner calm. Eyes on God and His plan not yours.

When others are afraid, you can have the presence of mind to take advantage of the turmoil swirling all around you. This state of mind allows you to be a leader, not a follower. To be the chess player, not the chess piece. To be one of the few who do, not one of the many who just talk!

But is it even possible to become unshakeable in these crazy times? Or is it just a pipe dream? Do you remember how you felt in 2008 when the financial crisis demolished the global economy? Do you remember the fear, the anxiety, the uncertainty that gripped us all when the world seemed to be falling apart?

In 2006 my small real estate team completed 400 transactions of lots, land, and homes. In 2008 we sold forty. I saw my world of real estate holdings dissolve and shrink in value and number over the next several years into a small fraction of what I had obtained.

Finally, in 2010 my business partner and I discovered our property manager had been embezzling a small fortune from our investment properties accounts. I was shaken to my very core. The future looked grim!

HOW TO FIND CERTAINTY IN AN UNCERTAIN WORLD.

What are you certain of and dependent upon in this world under the sun?

1. Job?
2. Money?
3. Retirement account?
4. Spouse?
5. Insurance?

We do not see reality; we see our thoughts. Thought creates our experience of the world. What holds many of us back is a feeling that we're in over our heads. It doesn't help that the world seems overwhelmingly complex. The following keys will lead us to become certain of some areas of our uncertain lives. These "I know for sure" things help us build strongholds that can withstand the storms ahead.

It Is Most Important to Set-Up These "Tents" Before the Storms!

1. **Prioritize our lives:** There are only one or two priorities in each area of your life, not ten. Any more than two and it becomes a list not a priority.
   a. Choose your priorities for each area of your life (one or two targets).
   b. Apply appropriate time to each "equity of your life" (not balanced or equal time, but appropriate time to meet the needs).
   c. Design and apply a system that will create habits to make these changes a normal part of your lifestyle (morning routine, affirmations, reading, practice, evaluate).

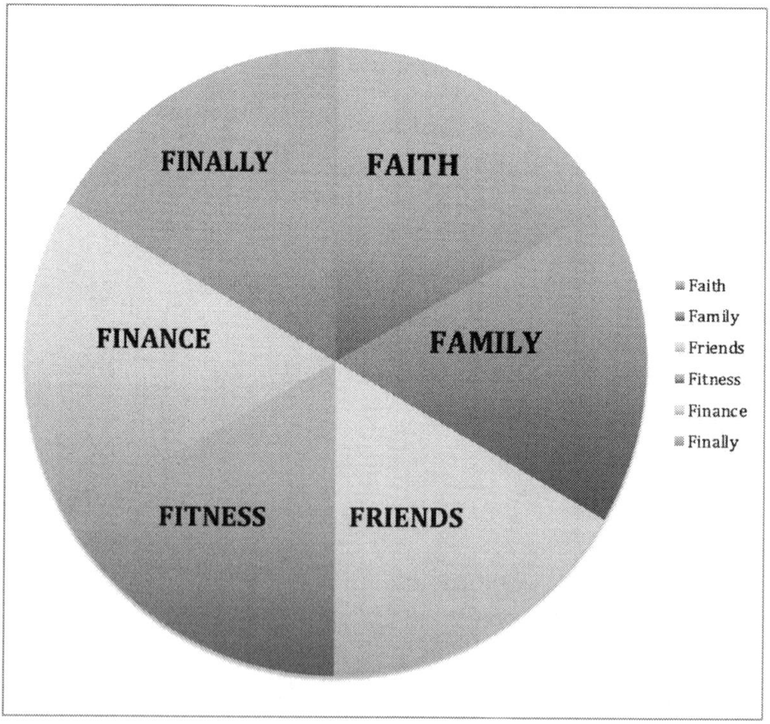

Some years ago, a friend experienced a big loss—thieves broke into his home and stole lots of valuables. Later, he was asked, "Did you cry?" to which he responded, "I don't cry for things that won't cry for me!"

What a profound lesson. We spend most of our lives in pursuit of material possessions, very often at a price of fewer human connections. Yet, at the end, when we are gone, our possessions will be silent, and we'll be missed only by the people who were closest to us. We came into this world with nothing and we will leave with nothing.

I wish you a healthy life-time where your biggest possessions will be a huge circle of family and friends.

2. **Master something!** We always get compensated for the value we bring to the marketplace. What is your "value proposition"? What are you better at than anyone else?
   a. What makes you different from the others that do what you do?
   b. What makes you "the best" in your craft or point of business? (People will always pay for "the best" and pay more for it. Lexus/Mercedes etc.)
   c. Master a shot that you know you can score when you need to (practice).

MOST PEOPLE SETTLE INTO ONE OF THREE AREAS: SURVIVAL, SUCCESS, OR SIGNIFICANCE.

If you're like many people, you may be struggling just to keep your head above water. You're in survival mode. Whether because of circumstances, setbacks, or poor choices, or bad diagnosis, you have to put a tremendous amount of effort into just making it day to day.

If you're working hard to make life better for yourself and your family, then I applaud you. Keep working. But once you've gotten to a place of stability, then what? What will you live for? Will you serve yourself or others? Will you put all of your energy into success, in trying to get farther ahead than others? Or, will you work toward significance? Will you try to make a difference by helping others get ahead?

Success Is Hard to Handle

Much of my career as a speaker and writer has focused on helping people who've already achieved a level of success to find true meaning in their lives. For some that's a fairly smooth transition. For others it's not. Many people I interact with have gotten to a place where they've reached some of their financial goals—or surpassed them—and they thought it would bring some kind of fulfillment.

They discover that they're still not satisfied. And in some cases, they are actually less fulfilled than when they started their journey. They went into their journey thinking, *If I get more for me, I'll be happier.* They thought it would bring them satisfaction and fulfillment, yet their lives feel hollow and empty.

Many people tie their significance to social position, their title, their net worth or bank balance, the car they drive, their prestigious address, the man or woman on their arm, or some other status symbol.

Their mentality is, "If I do enough and have enough, even if I am self-centered, it will bring fulfillment and happiness." The problem is that self-centeredness and fulfillment cannot peacefully co-exist. They're incompatible. They are opposites and oppose one another.

Sometimes, people struggling with this issue are uncertain about what to do. Often, they grapple with the idea of making a career change in their forties or fifties. When I encounter someone in this situation, I ask: "Do you really want to switch careers, or do you want to switch to a life that matters?"

The problem usually isn't the job or career. When people are self-centered, they can make external changes, and they won't be any happier in their next career. The grass only looks greener on the other side.

Instead, they need to shift to significance by putting other people first. Their thinking needs to change from what's in it for me? to what can I do for others? They must focus on God's plan and purpose. Until that change occurs, happiness, fulfillment, and significance will always be out of their reach.

That doesn't mean success is bad. The reality is that many people must achieve a certain amount of success before they're ready for significance and fulfillment. They need to have found themselves, achieved something before they have something to give to others.

3. **We are a physical and spiritual being.**

Natural Life versus Spiritual Life

Our natural reaction is to be so precise—trying always to forecast accurately what will happen next—that we look upon uncertainty as a bad thing. We think that we must reach some predetermined goal, by a predetermined time, but that's not the nature of the spiritual life.

Linear Thinking

The nature of the spiritual life is that we are certain in our uncertainty. Certainty is the mark of the commonsense life—gracious uncertainty is the mark of the spiritual life.

To be certain of God means that we are uncertain in all our ways, not knowing what tomorrow may bring. This is generally expressed with a sigh of sadness, but it should be an expression of breathless expectation. We are uncertain of the next step, but we are certain of God.

a. Practice and grow your faith.
b. Learn to listen and follow your "inner voice" the Holy Spirit, in every area of your life.
c. Invest some of your 1,440 minutes in prayer and fasting and worship.
d. Learn to become a better listener. It requires practice. Put others first and be generous to their needs. I have never regretted being generous.

In my daily battle fighting Parkinson's I am surrounded by uncertainty. I have good days and not so good days. My family and friends are sensitive to my actions and reactions and try to help where possible. After a three-year battle, I have concluded the following:

- Life is uncertain and not fair. It can change in a minute.
- Time, family, and friends are more important than money.
- Everything under the sun has an expiration date, except your Spirit.
- God is certain. He is the same yesterday, today, and tomorrow. He is your rock, your foundation, your refuge, and an ever-present help in a troubled world.
- Seek God first and he will add all the other stuff.

Prayer: Father, all of these things I know are true and I believe: Help my unbelief.

Chapter 24

COURAGE AND STRENGTH

"I can do all things through him who gives me strength."
Philippians 4:13 (NIV)

I fully understand that a bad diagnosis or tragic news requires courage and strength to power through and become an overcomer. It also requires support, a strong family, compassion, endurance, and a strong relationship with the Holy Spirit power.

I firmly believe that no one leaves this earth unscathed—everyone is somehow harmed, hurt, rejected, abused, and treated unfairly. No matter what your circumstance or challenge or past, I can easily find someone who is suffering or has suffered much worse.

I often hear people say Jesus was never anxious, surprised, caught off guard, or unaware. But I read where Jesus is often surprised at the disciples' inability to comprehend and understand or apply his lessons to themselves. "Are you still so dull?" he asked them more than once.

I take comfort knowing that my Lord Jesus suffered deeply within himself just like me. He knows and has experienced the troubles I am experiencing and even prayed for the challenge to pass by Him in Mark 14: 'They went to a place called Gethsemane, and Jesus said to his disciples, 'Sit here while I pray.' He took Peter, James and John along with him, and he began to be deeply distressed and troubled. 'My soul is overwhelmed with sorrow to the point of death,' he said to them. 'Stay here and keep watch.'

"Going a little farther, He fell to the ground and prayed that, if possible, the hour might pass from Him. '*Abba* Father,' He said, 'everything is possible for you. Take this cup from me. Yet not what I will, but what you will.' Mark 14:32-36 (NIV)

I, too, have prayed for healing from the evil disease of Parkinson's and said those words: "Father, everything is possible for you. Why have you allowed this to happen to me and will You snatch it from me in the name of Jesus!"

I have read healing scriptures every time I take my medicine. I have asked the Holy Spirit to reveal any sin, present or past that I may pray for forgiveness and repent to remove any barrier to God's blessing in my life. I have asked others to pray on my behalf for healing and I promised to give all the glory to him everywhere I go.

After all of that I now say, "Yet not what I will, but what you will." I know He knows what's best for me and I trust Him. I serve at His pleasure and work out His plans, not mine.

"Do not be anxious about anything, but in every situation, by prayer and petition, with thanksgiving, present your requests to God. And the peace of God, which transcends all understanding, will guard your hearts and your minds in Christ Jesus." Philippians 4:6-7 (NIV)

Let me ask you a question: What in your life are you doing that isn't under your own power? I mean, what are you doing that you couldn't do under your limited power, but you could only do under God's power?

If you are like most people the truth is nothing. We only take on what we can easily do or with little effort of our own power. Why? Do we believe we can do all things through Him who strengthens us? Do we believe God will do what He promised?

David didn't fight the giant with a nuclear weapon or high caliber, automatic machine gun. He killed him with a rock. Oh, and one other thing...God's power. David said that God has delivered for him in the past and He will deliver the giant to him as well. He believed it.

The Bible (and history) is full of Christians who had all kinds of supernatural powers such as:

- Ezekiel could "see" the future. Ezekiel 37: 1-14
- Samson could tear apart lions with his bare hands. Judges 14: 5-6
- Peter's shadow could perform faith healing miracles. Acts 5:15
- Elisha could part rivers by striking the water with torn clothing. Kings 2: 11-14
- Paul could bring people back to life. Acts 20:9-12
- Paul was immune to poisonous snake bites. Acts 28:3-6
- Moses had a magical staff. Exodus 7:10-12

Understand this, in the end times you can't fight the enemy with your own power. He is too powerful and you can't out-think evil. You must call on the power of God through the Holy Spirit. Don't go into battle until the power of the Holy Spirit to fall upon you.

CHAPTER 25

OUR BELIEFS DIRECT OUR PATHS!

"I believe I can do more, be more, have more. I am not afraid!"

For the next few minutes please pay no attention to me but pay close attention to my words. Think about how they might apply to your life!

So, you thought you would be further along in your life by now. You thought that the problems that plagued you early in life would be over by now. But you made some bad choices, a few mistakes, and poor decisions, and you have begun to believe that this is all you will be able to accomplish now.

You never believed this could happen to you—it wasn't in your plan and now you believe it's too late for you. You have to settle!

But I believe, that more success can be achieved by everyone. Success does not take into consideration where you come from, what you look like, how many mistakes you've made in the past, or anything else about your past. All that matters is what you believe. It does not matter what you did in the past; it matters only what you do at this moment—next. Move forward.

Say to yourself: "I believe I can do more, have more, be more. I am not afraid."

The Size of Your Success Is Determined By the Size of Your Belief

Your life always moves in the direction of your beliefs. What you believe matters! What your mind can conceive and believe, it can achieve! Good or bad.

Belief and Success: We take belief for granted. Belief gives us *hope!* You need to believe that anything and everything is possible. You need to believe that you *can* do *all* things through him who strengthens you. Philippians 4:13

Repeat after me: I can do ALL things!

The Ability to Believe: The ability to believe is a function of three variables.

1. **It is all about your mindset.** The more mindfully aware you are, the more you will believe in the things that advance you and disbelieve the "Weapons of Mass Distraction" that distract you.
2. **The second stage is the stronger you are, the more confident you become** and the more you are able to believe in yourself and be less afraid of the unknown. Without this strength, your fear will rise to the surface making you doubt yourself.
3. **Third is an honest evaluation of you.** You need to engage in self-audit of you. Be true to yourself about what you know, what you don't, and where your strength and weaknesses are. There must be this ability to see your-

self in truth and transparency. If you hide your shortfalls, there will always be a part of you that is uncertain of your footing because you know beneath the surface you're living a lie.

State of Belief

Your state of belief is not something you arrive at by accident. You have to guard your belief. As Henry Ford said, "Whether you think you can, or you think you can't, you're right."

The road to success has many detours and distractions. The following are a few of the most common ones. Belief is the best way to overcome them:

1. Self-doubt
2. Procrastination
3. Fear of Failure
4. Fear of Success
5. Pleasing Others
6. Excuses
7. Negative Thoughts
8. Negative Environment

Every single detour can be fatal to your success because of your failure to believe in your own abilities. You may even think that you are not worthy of success and that a mediocre life is all you will ever have. All of this is unbelief.

It's not what you think that's holding you back, it's what you think you are not.

Now, let's take a look in more detail at some of the challenges on our list above.

Self-Doubt: Self-doubt will throw you off your game, whether it's in a golf game or Olympic competition. It's a condition that sneaks up on you at the beginning of a battle and you question your entire existence and right to chase your dreams and goals.

Procrastination: Procrastination is opportunity's enemy. We must understand and employ the *power of now*! Live powerfully present every day. The best time to do something was yesterday. The next best time is now.

Fear of Failure: It's not failure itself that holds you back; it's the fear of failure that paralyzes you.

FEARS COME FROM OUR BELIEFS!

Belief is the strongest reaction you can have to any obstacle in your path.

Excuses: "Excuses are what you say when you quit or fall short. The biggest problem with excuses, it's that you let *yourself* down."

WHEN YOU BELIEVE SOMETHING CAN BE DONE, YOU WILL ACCOMPLISH IT.

Self-Belief: Your beliefs become your identity.

Rules to Believe:

- Intentions do not equal success.
- With God ALL things are possible.
- Belief matters.
- Self-Awareness is critical.
- TRUST yourself.

YOU BRAIN IS LIKE A LIGHT SWITCH: WHAT YOU BELIEVE DIRECTS YOUR ACTIONS.

If you were in a coma and suddenly awoke with no memory and you were told that you are a "Navy Seal," you would most definitely conduct yourself differently than if they told you that you are a "piano teacher." When you are unsure of what you truly believe or fall short because false belief you will never rise to your potential.

It has been said you'll believe it when you see it, but the truth is: Believe it, and you will see it.

BELIEF REQUIRES ACTION

Key Lessons:

- Learn how to change your beliefs and you can change your life.
- Learn how to change the limiting beliefs that continually sabotage our success.
- Remove the barriers to greater success—in your business and in your life.
- How our brain constructs beliefs and reinforces them (without you knowing it).

YOU ARE BORN WITH NO BELIEFS; BELIEFS ARE LEARNED!

- Learn to expose and change limiting beliefs that diminish, sabotage and control your life—determining your feelings of security, worthiness, self-image, capability, and competence.
- Learn how to believe in yourself, your abilities, and your potential.

Step 1: When you change your thinking, you change your beliefs.

Change begins with the mind. Beliefs are nothing more than a product of what you have thought, something that you have bought into—always remember that. What you believe, what you think, is just a collection of continual thoughts that have formed themselves into a conviction.

Step 2: When you change your beliefs, you change your expectations.

Belief is the knowledge that we can do something. It is the inner feeling that what we undertake, we can accomplish. For the most part, all of us have the ability to look at something and know whether we can do it. So, in belief there is power—our eyes are opened, our opportunities become plain, our visions become realities. Our beliefs control everything we do. If we believe we can or we believe we cannot, we are correct.

Step 3: When you change your expectations, you change your attitude.

Your expectations are going to determine your attitude. Most people get used to average; they get used to second best. The first and most important step toward success is the expectation that we can succeed.

Step 4: When you change your attitude, you change your behavior.

When our attitude begins to change, our behavior begins to change. The reason that we have to make personal changes is that we cannot take others on a trip that we have not made.

Step 5: When you change your behavior, you change your performance.

Many people would rather live with old problems than new solutions. We would rather be comfortable than correct; we would rather stay in a routine than make changes. Even when we know that the changes are going to be better for us, we often don't make them because we feel uncomfortable about making that kind of a change. Until we display courage and get used to living with something that is not comfortable, we cannot improve.

Step 6: When you change your performance, you change your life.

It is easier to turn failure into success than an excuse into a possibility. A person can fail, turn around and understand their failure to make it a success. But I want to tell you, a person who makes excuses for everything will never truly succeed. Don't you know some people who just have an excuse for everything? Why they could not, should not, did not, would not, have not, will not. I promise you, when you excuse what you are doing and excuse where you are, and you allow the exceptions, you fail to reach your potential. It is impossible to turn excuses into possibilities. NO EXCUSES!

Chapter 26

WHEN YOU STAY READY...YOU DON'T HAVE TO GET READY!

Blueprint for Success

Close your eyes for a moment and think about the greatest life you can imagine as you live an absolutely extraordinary life of success. Whether it's an amazing lifestyle, the home of your dreams, financial freedom, independence, charitable giving—whatever that dream looks like to you, picture yourself immersed in it right now. Just enjoy your hard-earned success for just a moment. Can you feel it?

That's the dream life. Then there's the reality. Open your eyes now. Honestly what does your day-to-day life look like? Not F-a-k-e-b o o-k! Not your social media posts complete with filters and make-up, but real authentic life. The real you, life conditions. If what you really see is worry, stress, or uncertainty, or if it simply isn't everything you want it to be, then this chapter is for you. This chapter is difficult but rewarding and real.

Are you happy about your current life condition or could it be improved? I heard a speaker teach on our mind and how it responds. He said, our mind is divided into two parts: "Thinker and Prover."

Thinker can think about anything it wants to. Then the prover must prove the thought, it has no other choice. It has to prove the thought is right. What you think about you will become. What you think about, you bring about. Thinking is vital to improving our life conditions and our very existence.

The Prover will take the thought and begin to search your memory and scan everything it finds to validate the thought. Such as times when you failed, quit, gave up or settled. The Prover will look in your past and present to prove the thought.

Then you will believe and enforce the information and conclude that you aren't capable of doing the thought but fail or settle for less. You become incapable. Whatever you think you are, you already are.

LIMITING BELIEFS: AS A MAN THINKETH SO HE BECOMES.

James Allen wrote a book in 1902 titled, *As a Man Thinketh,* which, in my opinion kicked off the self-help movement and has inspired and transformed many still today. I read it twice each year. It has made a dramatic change in my life for the better.

> "For he is the kind of person who is always thinking about the cost. 'Eat and drink,' he says to you, but his heart is not with you." Proverbs 23:7 (NIV)

What does the Prover prove? Whatever the Thinker thinks. Want to change the outcome? Change what you think!

What does "blueprint" mean in the Bible? The blueprint guides them. It reminds them of their foundation and shows them what to do next. It gives them a vision for the finished product. In the Christian life, we are not without a blueprint. God has given us a foundation and a plan for our lives in His Word.

"Be strong and very courageous. Be careful to obey all the law my servant Moses gave you; do not turn from it to the right or to the left, that you may be successful wherever you go. Keep this Book of the Law always on your lips; meditate on it day and night, so that you may be careful to do everything written in it. Then you will be prosperous and successful. Have I not commanded you? Be strong and courageous. Do not be afraid; do not be discouraged, for the LORD your God will be with you wherever you go." Joshua 1:7-9 (NIV)

People ask me, "What's it take to be truly happy?" I tell them it's one word: "Progress!" Have you ever been stuck in traffic and not moving at all for an extended time? How did you feel? It makes me frustrated and anxious. Then when we start moving, I feel better. Even moving at fifteen miles an hour I feel like I'm making progress and it changes my attitude. Life. It's about what you are becoming, not what you are getting! Keep progressing every day.

Sounds easy. What is easy to do is also hard to do consistently because we neglect too often. When we neglect a day, quitting is lurking around the corner. Some days we just don't feel like it. That is the day we need to do whatever it takes to keep progressing. Neglect is the first step to quitting. We have a limited number of days; don't waste even one. You can't afford it.

GREAT ADVICE: STOP MAJORING IN MINOR THINGS, YOU DON'T HAVE TIME.

Three words that will change your life: ***Get over it.***

You can't harbor resentment and play the blame game and still progress. It doesn't work, it only robs you of your happiness. Events in every equity of your life are the reflection of your responses, your thoughts, your own actions, and decisions.

I heard a story from a friend where his wife gave him the "silent treatment" for two days. He didn't know it! He thought they were getting along swimmingly. She wasn't nagging him or criticizing his actions or comments. He was loving it. When she discovered he didn't even know what she was doing, it only made his wife angrier. Usually, the one harboring resentment suffers the most.

The average person loses focus in the conscious mind every six to ten seconds.

We Are the Most Distracted Generation in the History of the World

What are your "Weapons of Mass Distraction?" While your conscious brain can't possibly keep track of all that stuff, your non-conscious brain can, and it does, nonstop, twenty-four hours a day, every day of your life. If your conscious brain is a lot more limited than you realized, your non-conscious brain is vastly more powerful than you have ever imagined.

Remember how often your conscious brain loses focus? Every six to ten seconds. Guess how often your non-conscious brain loses focus? Never. Not once. Not ever. Wow!

The power center of the brain is non-conscious. This is where the great bulk of perception happens; it is where your habits reside, where your accomplishments and achievements take root. Your conscious mind is what you use to define, articulate, and set goals.

But it's your non-conscious mind that follows through with all the dozens, hundreds, or millions of actions necessary to achieve those goals. When you create a clear, focused picture of what you want, this part of your brain kicks into high gear, and doesn't stop until it finds it for you.

It's called the reticular activating system (RAS). It's a bundle of nerves located in the brainstem. Its job is to filter out unnecessary information so the most important stuff can get through. Let me give you an example. Several years ago, I purchased an Infinity Q45 car. It was a seafoam green color. Now, I had never owned a green car or knew anyone with a green car. I rarely have even seen a green car. So, on my drive home, what color cars and trucks did I see the most? Green! I saw green vehicles everywhere. Why? Because I had been thinking about it all morning and searching my mind's history to discern all I could remember about green vehicles. The RAS kicked-in and shut down all the thousands of things entering my mind space and only focused on my most thought about subject, green cars.

We walk, tie our shoes, speak in one or several languages, type on our computers, and drive our cars, all without thinking. What's more, habits cover a good deal more ground than just these basic, physical routines.

When you think the same thing over and over, it eventually becomes a habit of thought. A habit of thought over time (and repetition) becomes an attitude or belief.

Power of Habit–Power of Belief

Beliefs are not necessarily "the truth" at all. (Remember, there was a time when everyone believed the earth was flat.)

Limiting beliefs are nothing more than specific neural patterns in your brain, thoughts that are so ingrained they have become automatic. They are not there because they are "the truth," they have simply been handed down from generation to generation. They are there because someone put them there. We are talking here about your limiting beliefs—your habits of thought, opinion, and attitude about the world around you, and especially your beliefs about you, about your life and your prospects for financial fulfillment.

It's been defined that by the time you're eighteen years old, you've heard, "No, you can't" an average of 150,000 times. You've heard, "Yes, you can" about 5,000 times. That's thirty NOs for every YES. That makes for a powerful belief of "I can't."

The biggest obstacle to most people's goals has nothing to do with any external conditions or factors. It is this: They don't believe it will happen or that it can be done. If you don't believe it will happen, it is almost guaranteed that it won't. You simply cannot achieve a goal that you do not believe you can achieve, because those beliefs live in that part of the brain that is running the show, even though we typically are not aware of it.

Here's the problem: Beliefs tend to be self-fulfilling. This is because habits are a thousand times stronger than desires. That is worth restating: not twice as strong, not even three times as strong, but a thousand times stronger.

You may have the desire to increase your income tenfold, but if your habits of thought do not expect anything like that to occur, it will be next to impossible for it to happen; you will take no lasting, productive action toward that goal. You can desire to lose weight and by will-power and desire do well for three weeks. You might even lose some weight which should reinforce your momentum. Then you wake-up one morning and you don't feel like eating clean and working out. It's just one day. You have done so well for three weeks and now you deserve a cheat day of doing what you want, doing what you "feel like" of desire: donuts and cheesecake for breakfast. It's only one day. So, you slip back into your old habits of poor diet and lack of exercise. It's called neglect and neglect is the first step to quitting.

It is your habits, not your desires or other conscious thoughts, that run your actions.

The biggest challenge facing America today is: We have lost or are losing our ability to think. I call it "Digital Dementia." Digital Dementia happens because we don't have to think any more and AI is making it easier to never think.

I was on a non-stop flight to Miami for a speaking engagement. Somewhere between Nashville and Miami I lost my cell phone. I looked everywhere and couldn't find it. The lady sitting next to me said she bet it was in my bag. I had already looked twice so I ignored her. I began to think: *Who was I supposed to meet at baggage claim for the car service…don't know…it's in my phone. And what time do I have to be at the venue for my first speaking session? Don't know, it's in my phone. Who is my point of contact for the event? Don't know… it's in my phone.*

Frustrated I sat back in my seat and took some deep breaths when my seat mate said, "I know it's in your bag. I lose stuff in my purse all the time. Just look again and check everywhere." Alright I'll look again. Guess what, the first place I looked, there it was. It had slipped between the cover of my small note binder. Relieved and a little embarrassed, I slowly reviewed all of the things I could not remember. Now I make a hard copy, a digital copy, I email myself a copy and I memorize all of the important information I will need during my event. I now think again.

I read where Dan Cathy of Chick-fil-A fame invests one hour per week, uninterrupted, of just him, a pad of paper, and a pen. Just thinking and writing down every thought regardless of relevance. Then later, he reviews all the ideas and chooses one of them to act upon either in his own life, his stores, or his community. All of this from a single thought.

Here is where you adopt new beliefs by focusing on them and repeating and retraining them till, they are impressed on the non-conscious part of your brain.

This is where you get off your butt and do something, it's not realistic to expect that much will happen if you don't … no matter how positive you are.

I Can. I Will. I Must! … Repeat!

You simply cannot achieve a goal that you do not believe you can achieve, because those beliefs live in that part of the brain that is running the show, even though we typically are not aware of it.

The next biggest obstacle to winning is you don't believe in you. To change your life conditions, you must:

- Change your habits.
- Watch. Listen. THINK. Act.
- Develop a plan and memorize it and practice it over and over until your non-conscious brain acts on it automatically.
- Repeat and adjust as needed.
- Never neglect the action plan.

Life is not fair and it's not as easy as I would prefer. At times life is messy and chaotic. Controlling your mind and including God will make everything easier and possible. You control you.

CHAPTER 27

YOU MUST BE PRESENT TO WIN

THE PRESENT

As the years have passed, I fully understand two things:

Time is more valuable than money. You can save money, but you can't save time. You can make more money, but you can't make more time. You can work a second job to gain more money, but you will lose more time. Time is fleeting. Make sure you are trading your precious time for something important. Don't waste time arguing, holding a grudge, being offended, jealous, or envious. Invest your time building relationship with our Heavenly Father, Lord Jesus, the Holy Spirit, and your family and friends; they are more valuable than all the money on earth. Remember you came into this physical world with nothing and you will leave with nothing.

You must live in the present. Yesterday is gone. You can't change anything about yesterday except to learn from it in order to live a better life today, in the present. We are not promised tomorrow. We only have the here and now. Embrace the present. Live in the moment. Give others your undivided attention. They need to know what you have already learned. Matthew 6:34 says, "Therefore do not worry about tomorrow, for tomorrow will worry about itself. Each day has enough trouble of its own." (NIV) So, yesterday is gone and tomorrow isn't promised, all we have is today. Don't wait until you get that job promotion or the kids get out of school or when you retire … do it now!

Living in the present is a powerful way to deal with life more and enjoy more of your life. I was guilty of thinking about my family and the plans for the weekend while I was at work and supposed to be focused on my job. When I was home, I would be thinking about work, checking my texts and emails. I also would be planning our vacation while at work or home to the smallest detail. Then while I was on vacation, I would be thinking about work again and even called to check-in. No wonder I stayed so tired; in my mind I was always traveling.

It's not enough to just be present physically; you must also be present mentally. I have personally experienced being with my family physically while my mind was somewhere else. I was thinking through all the changes happening to me physically because of the Parkinson's disease. I sat at dinner and I could see my family talking to me, but I couldn't focus enough to fully hear them. My mind was aflush with *What-if* and *Why me, why now?* This is not being present. You must be present to win.

To be present requires discipline and focus. I understood that I would have good day where I felt symptom free; I was the old me and loved every minute of it. It was easy to be present and all was well in the world. I also knew that some days would be not so good. I experienced sleepless nights, spasms, and dizziness when standing or walking.

One good and one not so good day. Then sometimes I would have several good days in a row before a not so good day would show up. Then I had a second bad day and then a third. I went from saying "Tomorrow has to be a good day," to "No … another bad day." My mind began thinking, *Am I ever going to have another good day? I haven't slept much; will I ever sleep well again?* From there I played the victim card and was grumpy with people and my family. No matter how hard I tried, I just couldn't change my trajectory. I tried harder and harder, but no change. It's not easy to be present when you feel miserable and who wants to be around you anyway.

Then it hit me; with man this is impossible, but with God all things are possible. I was fighting the enemy with my limited strength and not the power of the Almighty. So, I called on His power and commanded the enemy to leave me alone. He has no power over me and no part in me.

Next, I began to praise God for the victory. I repented for not including Him in my plans and praised Him some more and the enemy had to flee. Then something wonderful happened. I had a really good day and another one the next day. Several days in a row, many of my symptoms subsided and diminished. His power is so much more effective than mine.

Have you ever noticed that you can water your lawn with a hose or irrigation for several days in a row and it doesn't compare to a few hours of rain from heaven? God's ways and power is different from everything else we experience. We should always seek His power for every detail of our lives. Make it a habit to include Him in our daily life. He will deliver to us that which we are seeking. God is able and faithful.

While I've been writing this book, I was notified that my little brother had passed away. Even though he has been in extremely poor health battles the last four years, the news still took me by surprise. It caused me to pause and reflect on him and all the memories of him. Growing up and even into adulthood we were complete opposites. We disagreed a lot and the many times the medical staff said he didn't have long; I went to visit him (he was in Indiana and I am in Nashville area) to discuss eternity. Most of the time it ended up with us disagreeing. About eighteen months ago, I was visiting with him and of course the salvation discussion took place before I was leaving. To my welcome surprise, he said he wanted to accept Jesus and become a child of God. I couldn't believe my ears. What was different? Why now not the other times we discussed it?

Wasting no time, we had a brief conversation to insure we were in full understanding of what was about to take place. We prayed together and his facial expression and demeanor changed instantly. We both teared up and talked some more on being a new creature and a child of God. It was a time of belief for me because while I never gave up, in my heart I thought he would never accept the Lord and would maybe die before he got to. I learned everything is in God's timing and not ours. Never quit, never give up.

Every visit after that my brother wanted to pray the prayer all over again and talk about being a child of God. We discussed what eternity would be like and how he would have a glorified body and there would be no more pain. How we would see mom and dad and others again. We ended our visit in total agreement. God still performs miracles if we endure, believe, and don't give up.

Fast forward to last week and the news of my brother passing from "time under the sun" to "time under the Son" and how relieved I was in knowing he was in a better place. Knowing he is with Jesus in Paradise left me feeling joyful and not sad. I'm sad he is no longer with us here on Earth, but I'm celebrating he is with our King, the one and only living God. The lesson of the story is to take advantage of now and learn to become powerfully present.

I'd like to remind you that this book is not hypothetical or academic theory, but real-life experience that works every time and every place you apply it. You can become an overcomer. It requires endurance, perseverance, and closer relationship with God. Being an overcomer is far superior than being overcome. No matter your current life condition under the sun, it can, it will, and it must get better if you overcome.

It also requires training not just trying. Imagine being taken to the hospital emergency room with severe stomach pain. A physician examines you and runs a bunch of tests to determine what's wrong. The doctor comes in and explains the results to you, "We think you have this and that but we are not 100 percent sure. So, I want to operate on you to see exactly what's going on inside there. Once I have you open, I'm sure I can determine what to do and get you healthy again. I will try my best and my best is really good."

The medical team leave to prepare for your surgery and all the paperwork required. Alone with your thoughts another physician comes in and says he has reviewed your file and he 100 percent knows what your problem is and he is 100 percent convinced that he can fix it. He goes on to introduce himself and he is the foremost expert on this procedure. He has trained for the last ten years to perfect this surgery and he has completed 300 of these procedures with a 100 percent success rate. And he also teaches the procedure at residency programs around the world and is considered the world expert.

The only question for you is who do you choose? Will you select the first doctor who will try his best and his best is really good? Or will you take the second doctor who has trained for ten years and performed 300 successful surgeries and even teaches the procedure around the world?

TRYING VERSUS TRAINING.

Well, of course we would select the highly trained doctor. Simple and obvious answer for anyone. But look at life under the sun. So many of us want to learn enough to slide by while we try our best. Training is long hard work. Training requires studying, practicing, being evaluated and certified so others know the sacrifices you made to be an expert.

I've learned no matter how hard I try; I am still limited on my results and future improvement. However, the more I train the better I become and the more I can help, provide for, and solve problems. The more value I can bring to the marketplace and my community. You will have to overcome a lot of challenges and obstacles but you can do it. Don't just try—train.

This book is coming to an end, but your life is not. Read and re-read this book so you may soak it in and act on it when needed. Give a copy or recommend it to anyone suffering a bad health diagnosis, tragic news, or severe family challenge.

Remember it's not what you can get, it's what you are becoming—OVERCOMER!

You have everything you need to succeed till the end, but it will take everything you have!

Made in the USA
Columbia, SC
07 December 2023

27964317R00093